KITCHENER

"Kitchener's Enterprises"
by Richard Pearce

Windsor Publications, Ltd.
Burlington, Ontario

KITCHENER

A Tradition of Excellence

A
Contemporary
Portrait
by
Ray
Stanton

Windsor Publications, Ltd.—Book Division
Managing Editor: Karen Story
Design Director: Alexander D'Anca
Photo Director: Susan L. Wells
Executive Editor: Pamela Schroeder

Staff for *Kitchener: A Tradition of Excellence*
Manuscript Editor: Douglas P. Lathrop
Photo Editor: Larry Molmud
Editor, Corporate Profiles: Melissa W. Patton
Production Editor, Corporate Profiles:
    Justin Scupine
Proofreader: Michael Moore
Co-ordinator, Corporate Profiles:
    Gladys McKnight
Editorial Assistants: Elizabeth Anderson,
    Kate Coombs, Lori Erbaugh,
    Phyllis Feldman-Schroeder, Kim Kievman,
    Michael Nugwynne, Kathy B. Peyser,
    Theresa J. Solis
Publisher's Representative, Corporate Profiles:
    Maya Hart
Layout Artist, Corporate Profiles: C.L. Murray
Layout Artist, Editorial: Ellen Ifrah
Designer: Christina L. Rosepapa

Windsor Publications, Ltd.
Elliot Martin, Chairman of the Board
James L. Fish III, Chief Operating Officer
Mac Buhler, Vice President/Acquisitions

ISBN: 0-89781-381-2

**RIGHT: Feathery residents
of Victoria Park accept
snacks from their visitors.
Photo courtesy First Light**

**PG. 8/9:Curious cows
examine a photographer's
behavior. Photo by Dave
Prichard/First Light**

**PG. 100/101: Mennonite
men amble alongside a
rural road in Waterloo
County. Photo by Ken
Straiton/First Light**

PART 2

KITCHENER'S ENTERPRISES

RIGHT: Photo by Dave Prichard/First Light

1

FROM BERLIN TO KITCHENER

Joseph Schoerg and Samuel Betzner surveyed the vast wilderness before them. The densely forested landscape was dominated by a collection of large sand hills and several large swamps. Devout Christians that they were, Schoerg and Betzner were surely reminded of the land God gave to Cain. But the trees told a different story. Oak, maple, hickory, beech, and black walnut grew strong and tall, a familiar sign of rich soil which called to mind one word—Pennsylvania.

When the two pioneers first viewed the area in 1800, they knew they had found a home. Mennonites of German background, they were seeking a fresh start away from the uncertainties of life in their native Pennsylvania. Their pacifist ideals had prevented them from taking sides in the Revolutionary War and, like many other Mennonites, they no longer felt welcome in the United States. They were not concerned by the land's lack of amenities; instead, they were impressed by its isolation and fertility. In short, it was a perfect place for a Mennonite colony to take root and grow. Kitchener owes its very existence to the forbear-

1 BEYOND THE SAND HILLS

The Berliner Journal *was the German-language newspaper in Berlin at the turn of the century.*
Courtesy, Mrs. Bill Moyer

ance and assiduousness of these pioneers and their brethren.

Within two years 25 Mennonite families had joined Schoerg and Betzner, clearing the land and establishing small farms. In 1802 the nascent community was thrown into a state of shock when the settlers learned their deeds to the land were worthless. It appeared that Richard Beasley, the land speculator from whom they had purchased their homesteads, never held clear title to the land before selling it. But despite a considerable body of circumstantial evidence, Beasley never knowingly misled the settlers—he simply misunderstood to whom his mortgage payments should be directed. He nevertheless survives in local legend as an unscrupulous confidence man. The business life of what would become a very successful and highly industrialized community was off to a decidedly shaky start.

To make matters worse, the settlers soon found themselves in financial difficulties of their own making. Like Beasley, they tried to pay their mortgages with proceeds from land sold to new settlers. To their dismay, when the mortgage came due in 1805, they were still far from their goal and unable to pay the balance.

Returning to Pennsylvania, a group of pioneers appealed to their fellow Mennonites for help and struck a resonant chord. While few agreed to move, 26 recognized the business opportunity before them and formed an investment group called the German Company to finance the purchase of the Beasley Tract. The foundation upon which Kitchener would prosper and grow was firmly in place. The 60,000 acres of primeval forest, swamps, and sand hills—called the German Company Tract—was surveyed and divided into farms of 448 acres each and allocated by lottery to prevent any shareholders from acquiring a portfolio of the most saleable land. Between 1805 and 1807 many Pennsylvania German families emigrated to the settlement. Two who came in 1807, Benjamin Eby and Joseph Schneider, would have a lasting impact on the community—Schneider as a farmer, miller, and founder of what would become Kitchener, and Eby as a preacher, Men-

Berlin's market house, completed by community leader Jacob Y. Shantz in 1869, was an enlarged farmer's market located at the rear of the Berlin Town Hall. Courtesy, Jean Moyer

nonite bishop, and elder statesman.

Commenting in 1824 on conditions in Upper Canada, author J. Howison advised prospective settlers seeking a homestead site to seriously consider "the goodness of the land, its dryness, the existence of a spring of water upon it, its vicinity to a road, a navigable river, a mill, a running stream, a market and an extensive and increasing neighbourhood." When Joseph Schneider chose his lot on what would become Queen Street, much of the land was low and wet, some was high and sandy, the nearest grist mill was at Dundas, there was no major road, the Grand River was several miles away, and the stream cutting across the property did not promise great water power. There was no market to speak of and the community was still quite small. Yet Schneider's land proved a catalyst for settlement and soon formed the hub of a thriving community.

As the settlement grew, the inhabitants began to replace their first crude log cabins with frame homes. At first the lumber came from Abraham Erb's mill in neighbouring Waterloo, but by 1816 Joseph Schneider had constructed a mill of his own, using the power generated by damming the creek on his property. In 1820 he used timber cut from the medieval trees growing on his farm to build a large home for his family. Carefully restored as a heritage landmark and museum, it still stands 170 years later as Kitchener's oldest structure.

Like Joseph Schneider, Benjamin Eby was a natural leader. When he arrived in 1807, the settlers, being very devout Christians, worshipped in their homes. He took it upon himself to preach the gospel, and began his ministry in 1809. He became a bishop in 1812 and by 1813 had overseen construction of a church in which he also taught school, using the Bible as a textbook. The tiny community was soon known throughout the countryside as "Ben Eby's" and later "Ebytown." While the initiative of Joseph Schneider laid the foundation of business development in the community, Benjamin Eby established a strong spiritual and social tradition—a tradition which remains evident in the churches and schools of Kitchener.

As Eby and Schneider were setting high standards for the growth of the young settlement, the Industrial Revolution was beginning to play havoc with the craftsmen of Europe. Their talents rendered irrelevant by machines, many gifted artisans saw North America as a place of advancement. The German character and untapped market of a place like Ebytown suited displaced Germans perfectly.

Ebytown experienced a large influx of German immigrants between 1825 and 1835. Possessing a variety of trades, they lived quite literally by the German proverb, "Drive not thy nail into the air." W.V. Uttley elaborated upon this in his 1937 *History of Kitchener*, noting that "where other Canadians set out shade trees, they planted fruit trees; where others placed shrubs, they raised vegetables; and while others played games, they tilled their gardens." Ebytown, tradition of hard work and perseverance, embraced the energetic immigrants enthusiastically.

While the commercial life of Kitchener began with Joseph Schneider's mill in

1816, urban life in the modern sense of the word began around 1820 when Phineas Varnum, recognizing the need for a blacksmith shop and a roadhouse, persuaded Joseph Schneider to lease him a parcel of land at a point where Schneider's Road (now Queen Street) crossed the road to Dundas. By 1833 the community had a German language newspaper, the *Canada Museum und Allgemeine Zeitung.* While its original audience was extremely small, a scant two years later the paper noted with evident enthusiasm that "Berlin is in a flourishing position with all kinds of diligent tradesmen: among them a maker of spinning wheels and chairs, a hat maker, four cabinet makers and carpenters, one blacksmith, three stores, two shoemakers, a weaver, tailor, mason, wagon maker, hotel keeper and a doctor." Soon names like Frederick Gaukel, Jacob Hailer, and John Hoffman were as well known as those of Eby and Schneider. And the industrial diversity which remains the key to the economic success of the community was firmly in place.

The immigrants came from many different parts of Germany and their traditions were soon woven into the social fabric of the settlement, which was named Berlin in their honour. They proved Howison wrong by providing the skills, products, and keen business sense to overcome the geographic obstacles and complete the transformation from farm community to industrial centre.

In 1845 John Hoffman brought a steam engine and boiler over clay roads from Buffalo, New York. The machine was used to power a furniture factory on King Street. Soon Noah Ziegler was operating a steam-driven furniture factory several blocks away. Reinhold Lang, a native of Baden, Germany, built a tannery at the corner of King and Ontario streets in 1849. Soon afterward Louis Breithaupt, who had brought his family from New York at the outset of the American Civil War, established a tannery. Like Lang, his descendants would be leaders in the community for many years. Henry Bowman operated a foundry and George Rebscher opened the first lager brewery in Canada—selling his product for two shillings per gallon.

William Lyon Mackenzie King, seated next to the driver, became Member of Parliament for North Waterloo in 1908, the year this photo was taken. Courtesy, Mrs. Bill Moyer

In politics, Berliners tended to support Reform party candidates rather than the more conservative government candidates. In 1837, when leading Reformer William Lyon Mackenzie led an unsuccessful rebellion against the government and was forced to flee to the United States, some Berliners helped him on his way toward the border and freedom. Mackenzie's daughter, Isabella, would later marry

Berlin lawyer John King. One son, William Lyon Mackenzie King, was elected Member of Parliament for North Waterloo in 1908, succeeding the famous Waterloo distiller Joseph Emm Seagram, Conservative M.P. since 1896.

King served as Minister of Labour in the government of Sir Wilfrid Laurier and, although rejected by his home town in the reciprocity election of 1911, became leader of the Liberal Party in 1919. He was elected Prime Minister of Canada in 1921 and held that post longer than any person before or since. His boyhood home at Woodside is preserved as a National Historic Park.

The shrewd politics for which King became famous were part of Berlin's character from the very beginning, and in many ways the ability of Berliners to win their arguments ensured that the community would become a centre of importance. The establishment of a post office, seen as the mark of a community's significance, was the first step. For a time the nearest mail depot had been at Dundas. In 1827 neighbouring Galt was granted an office. Waterloo followed suit in 1831. Not to be outdone, Preston received the same designation in 1837. Outraged Berliners petitioned the government and were granted a post office of their own in 1842. For the first time Berlin was officially recognized as the equal of its neighbours. Of course, without such recognition the business life of Berlin would have been severely restricted.

In 1849, when Berliners heard of a proposal to create smaller counties in the newly united Province of Canada, some leading citizens ambitiously sought to have Berlin named the county seat. Galt also aspired to the same status but had a more legitimate claim to the prize. Already an incorporated village of 2,200, it was nearly large enough to be granted town status. Despite the fact that Berlin, with a population of only 508, was not even an incorporated village, representatives of the hamlet prodded, cajoled, and argued until the government decided that it should be the administrative centre of Waterloo County. While the verdict enraged the people of Galt, it touched off a huge celebration in Berlin. It was a tremendous boost to local businesses to be at the political centre of the county.

In 1854 Berlin celebrated its elevation to village status. Dr. John Scott, already reeve of Waterloo County, won the election as reeve in his home village. Two years later a branch line of the Grand Trunk Railway was built to Berlin, provid-

J.M. Schneider built his basement sausage business into one of Canada's largest meat-packing companies. Courtesy, Mrs. Bill Moyer

ing immediate access to Toronto. Berlin became ever more attractive as an industrial location. Factory sites along the railway were surveyed, and the King Street business district received a boost from the relatively easy access to a large and expanding market. Known for its economic diversity even in the 1850s, Berlin welcomed any and all new businesses. Abram Tyson opened a department store and Frederick Snyder built a block on King Street to house his stove and tinware business. Henry Bowman, already the owner of a foundry, built a block on King Street that housed a variety of businesses in the next two decades. Peter Hymmen, a tinsmith, made everything from suits of armor to jelly molds resembling different animals. August Fuchs, father of renowned nineteenth-century violinist George Fox, made and sold jewellery and watches. Architect John Kimmel saw little need for his services and opened a grocery store. Samuel Date founded the hardware business which grew to become C.N. Weber Limited.

In the 1860s William Niehaus, William Simpson, and Henry Bornhold competed as shoemakers. John Bramm ran a brickyard. Henry S. Boehmer opened a dry-goods store in 1868, while August and Charles Boehmer founded a hardware business; by 1874, however, they had begun to manufacture paper

Still unpaved in 1912, King Street, with streetcar rails down its centre, is shown in front of the Walper House. Courtesy, Mrs. Bill Moyer

boxes. There were many other businesses: clothing stores, flour and feed mills, butchers, monument makers, tailors, lumber dealers, even a lunch room.

Berlin was accorded town status in 1870 and divided into wards for the first time. Unlike other communities, where ward boundaries were often determined by the social standing of the residents, Berlin's were not. Factories and the homes of workmen could be found in every ward. Dr. William Pipe defeated John Fennell and railwayman H.F.J. Jackson to become the new town's first mayor.

The Kitchener City Hall, designed by William H.E. Schmalz and constructed in 1923, became the focal point of the community. Courtesy, Mrs. Bill Moyer

To encourage further industrial development, Berlin adopted a factory policy in 1874. The result was a burst of activity that flew in the face of the economic depression then gripping Canada. A five-year tax exemption and an annual bonus equal to the value of any rented premises were offered to any industrialist who chose to establish a business employing more than 75 men in Berlin. This incentive prompted Jacob Kaufman to open a planing mill on King Street near the railway in 1877. Although he was ridiculed for locating so far out in the country, his mill grew rapidly, and his involvement in a number of different businesses earned him the name, "Industrial Wizard." Like Lang and Breithaupt before him, his family would have a large and lasting impact on the community.

A board of trade was formed in 1886 through the efforts of pioneer industrialist Jacob Y. Shantz. Hardware merchant John Fennell became the first president, allowing Shantz to return to his other endeavours. Among other things, he ran the Dominion Button Works and was instrumental in the establishment of Mennonite colonies in Manitoba. As a contractor in Berlin, he built a market building behind the town hall in 1869. The market, although in a different building, has become one of Kitchener's most outstanding attractions.

In 1902, when Toronto began to investigate the possibility of deriving its electrical power from Niagara Falls, E.W.B. Snider of Waterloo advanced the idea that hydro power would be a boon to industry in Waterloo County. Surprisingly, his idea did not meet with wide support and would have died had it not been for the efforts of Berliner D.B. Detweiler. Together, the two visionaries began an intensive campaign for support which culminated on October 11, 1910, when

Press room workers at the Kitchener Daily Record posed for a group portrait in the paper's old Duke and Queen street building about 1929. Courtesy, Kitchener-Waterloo Record

Ontario Premier Sir James Whitney, accompanied by Hydro Commissioner Sir Adam Beck, threw a switch inaugurating the age of hydro-electric power in Ontario. Berlin itself was outfitted in decorations befitting a national holiday, and as the switch was thrown a specially prepared billboard was lit with electricity to reveal the motto, "Power for the People." That Berlin was the first municipality to receive hydro symbolized the importance of industry and innovation to Berliners.

On June 9, 1912, Berlin became a city. In a special publication entitled *Celebration of Cityhood,* a creed appeared summing up the philosophy of Berlin's business leaders:

I believe in Berlin. I love her as my home. I honor her institutions. I rejoice in the abundance of her resources. I have unbounded confidence in the ability and enterprise of her people, and I cherish exalted ideas of her destiny among cities of the Dominion. Anything that is produced in Berlin, from Canadian materials, by the application of Canadian brain and labor, will always have first call with me. And it's only good business on my part that it should.

This high-sounding rhetoric was obviously intended to make sure that Berliners realized that their standard of living depended upon the continued success of local businesses.

Newspapers in centres like Toronto, Montreal, Hamilton, Guelph, St. Thomas, St. Catharines, and Brantford were unanimous in their praise of Berlin and Berliners. The editor of the *Galt Reporter* was less flattering, however, noting that, "about the nearest thing to perpetual motion is the wagging of the Berliner's tongue in laudation of his own town." Clearly, the success of upstart Berlin did not sit well with the Galtonians.

The warm feelings of cityhood soon turned cold, however, when events in Europe plunged the world into the most devastating war it had ever seen. Unfortunately for Berlin, being Canada's German capital was no longer a source of pride, and the "Made in Berlin" trademark became a decided disadvantage for local businesses. In fact, citizens of British heritage often were openly hostile toward their German neighbours. In Ottawa Member of Parliament W.G. Weichel took the extraordinary step of guaranteeing Berlin's loyalty to the nation.

On one famous occasion a bust of Germany's Kaiser Wilhelm was removed from its pedestal in Victoria Park and unceremoniously tossed into the park lake by anti-German vandals. Some leaders of the German community suffered abuse and such indignities as having to kiss the British flag or sing "God Save The King" in public.

As the war dragged on, the situation in Berlin grew more tense. It became common for Muellers to suddenly become Millers and for Schmidts to become Smiths. Finally, a group of citizens persuaded the provincial government that the city's name had to be changed. A relieved council acted immediately, discussing and quickly abandoning a list of names that included such strange suggestions as Bercana (a peculiar combination of Berlin and Canada) Renoma, Dunard, Huronto, Agrioloeo, and Hydro City. A second, more acceptable list was then drawn up featuring Adanac, Benton, Brock, Corona, Keowana and Kitchener—the latter being added only after the dramatic and well-publicized death of British Secretary of War Lord Horatio Herbert Kitchener. The voting took four days, with Kitchener defeating Brock by a mere 11 votes. But significantly, 93 percent of eligible voters refused to cast a ballot.

In those heady pre-war years the "Made in Berlin" trademark had been a source of considerable pride for the community. Now, with a new name, Kitchener set about establishing a new, more acceptable, and modern identity. But one thing remained constant: a solid and diverse industrial foundation. King Street continued as the area's primary commercial thoroughfare and the architecture of the downtown slowly began to take on a distinctly twentieth-century look. The new century also brought new technology, and a variety of new and exciting businesses took root and grew.

Berlin's early emphasis on the furniture industry earned it the name "Grand Rapids of Canada." (Grand Rapids, Michigan, was an important furniture centre.) In the first decades of the twentieth century, Kitchener was regarded as the "Akron of Canada" in reference to the rubber businesses of that Ohio city. In 1899 George Schlee and Jacob Kaufman founded the Berlin Rubber Company. Later, one of their employees, T.H. Reider, formed the Merchants Rubber Company. In 1907 The Canadian Consolidated Rubber Company (later the Dominion Rubber Company) absorbed the two local businesses. A former Merchants employee, A.R. Kaufman, used the financial help of his father Jacob to immediately establish the Kaufman Rubber Company. Only 22 years old, he had begun a career that would see him become Kitchener's leading citizen.

J.M. Schneider possessed the same drive and ambition. Laid off due to

This aerial view of downtown Kitchener in 1959 shows the city hall and its cenotaph memorial. Courtesy, Mrs. Bill Moyer

injuries sustained at the Dominion Button Works, he began to make and sell sausages simply to earn a living. Although he returned to work, he soon opted to open a butcher shop. His tiny venture became Kitchener's largest business, and his products are well known throughout North America.

The stories of Kaufman and Schneider represent but two of Kitchener's many twentieth-century successes. Both were astute businessmen and both ensured that they always gave back to the community that had helped them prosper. Many others learned from them, followed their lead, and established for modern Kitchener the type of business environment advanced by the Mennonite pioneers many years before.

Kitchener became the first Ontario municipality to create a planning commission under the Ontario Planning and Development Act. W.H. Breithaupt was its first chairman. He was succeeded by A.R. Kaufman, who served for nearly four decades. The city's first urban plan, drawn by Thomas Adams and Horace Seymour, was approved by council in 1925 and provided a framework through which the community hoped to expand and prosper. Care was taken to ensure that residential areas would develop in harmony with industry and that the existence of one in an area would not necessarily preclude the existence of the other. When the Great Depression began in 1929, Kitchener was just beginning to recover from the turmoil of the Great War and was looking to the future with an enthusiasm lacking since 1914.

The *Kitchener Daily Record* took an informal poll of local industrialists at the outset of the Depression and concluded that "business is inherently sound and there is no substantial reason to believe that the winter period ahead will be more perplexing or difficult than in any former year." They were wrong. Although the city's famous industrial diversity prevented much of the chaos that plagued other communities, most industries were hit very hard. Revenue in the furniture industry alone fell from $11 million in 1928 to $1 million in 1932.

Although 4,500 Kitchener residents lived on relief at the height of the Depression, many kept their jobs and were able to sustain their families through the lean years. Relief payments were consistently higher than regular provincial

levels. By 1936, when the worst was over, local industries began to grow stronger and expand as they had done in the mid-1920s. They quickly returned to pre-Depression levels of productivity. The recovery received a tremendous boost in economic terms when World War II began, creating a boom in Kitchener unparallelled in its history.

Having learned a bitter lesson only 25 years before, Kitchenerites did all they could to support the war effort. From volunteering for active service to working long overtime shifts in essential industries, Kitchener people clearly demonstrated their patriotism. Any lingering damage from World War I had faded into the background by the time Hitler's Germany fell in 1945. Contracts poured into Kitchener for goods ranging from tires and trucks to food and electronics.

As in the first decades of the twentieth century, the post-war era was characterized by a dizzying number of technological advances and a corresponding broadening of Kitchener's industrial base. Automobile parts and electronics became extremely important parts of the city's economic superstructure. But as some traditional industries grew, others diminished or vanished altogether. The Breithaupt Leather factory closed in 1950 after nearly 100 years in business. The button industry was obliterated by foreign competitors and the Lang tannery, falling victim to changing technology and competition, closed in 1954. But the booming footwear, furniture, shirtmaking, and meatpacking industries took up the slack. More space was needed for housing, and efficient planning of a first-rate road network became a top priority. The automobile, a luxury for many in the 1920s and 1930s, became a necessity. A number of new schools were built, more space was required at the local hospitals, and the Kitchener Memorial Auditorium became an important fixture in the cultural and recreational development of the community.

In the 1950s a series of brochures were published extolling the virtues of locating a business in Kitchener. A booklet entitled "City of Talent" was published to mark the 1954 centennial of Berlin becoming a village. The booklet noted: "Industry in the sense of hope, hard work and perseverance was the mar-

Doing a job that was certainly hard on the back and feet, female employees of Merchant's Rubber Company assembled footwear while standing. Courtesy, Mrs. Bill Moyer

row of Kitchener's pioneers and out of high quality came small businesses and small factories that in less than a century were to be numbered among the best known and the soundest in Canada." The pride which characterized "Busy Berlin" had returned, helping Kitchener's industries return to the place of prominence their quality products earned for them.

Canada's first superhighway, Highway 401, was opened in 1960. Running from the Quebec border near Montreal to the U.S. border at Windsor, it became known as "Ontario's main street." It certainly provided Kitchener businesses easy access to markets in Ontario and the U.S. Indeed, it is often noted that within a 150-mile radius of Kitchener live more people than the entire population of Canada. Kitchener's pattern of development began to change as access to Highway 401—instead of to the railway, as in the past—became a priority in selecting a business location. The opening of Fairview Park Mall in 1965 changed the shopping habits of consumers and prompted a re-evaluation of the downtown core's role in the community. The mall's strategic location near Highway 401 drew shoppers from other communities as well as from the downtown shopping area. These developments precipitated a program of urban renewal that has continued into the 1990s.

In 1965 Canada signed the Automotive Trade Agreement with the U.S., and Kitchener became an important manufacturer of automotive parts. Budd Automotive, Lear Siegler, Uniroyal, and B.F. Goodrich expanded, opening up thousands of jobs. A 1973 ranking of the top Canadian companies by the *Financial Post* showed both Budd Automotive and J.M. Schneider, Inc., in the top 100. Carl Pollock's Electrohome grew so quickly that, for a time, it displaced both Schneiders and the rubber companies as the community's largest employer. The space age presented yet another challenge as Kitchener businesses sought new ways to perform old tasks using computers and advanced forms of robotics.

While Kitchener continued to expand, planners created industrial parks as attractive locations for businesses. Such initiatives were linked with the desire to control air and water pollution and to keep industries away from residential areas. Parks and open spaces were planned as recreation areas. A pedestrian mall was planned for the downtown, with a link to nearby Victoria Park. High-rise offices and residential properties would modernize the core area while providing attractive living and working environments. While many aspects of the 1965 downtown plan were implemented, it had become clear by 1970 that top priority should be given to making the downtown competitive with suburban shopping malls.

In 1971 a plan by Oxlea Investments to replace Kitchener's city hall square and market building with an office tower and shopping mall created a major controversy. In the most hotly contested referendum since the 1916 name change, 15,689 residents voted in favour of the project, against 11,513 in favor of maintaining the status quo.

Plans for a city centre on Mackenzie King Square continued with construction of the Centre in the Square in the late 1970s. World-class acoustics and excellent sight lines made it one of Canada's premier theatre-concert halls. Nevertheless, by the mid-1980s the revitalization of the downtown core had become the dominant issue. City council voted in favour of a new city hall and civic square located right on King Street. A national architectural competition was held to select a design which would "reflect the values of this vibrant community with its multi-cultural roots, industriousness and progressive economy, stability, friendliness, pride in the past and confidence in the future."

In the late 1980s Kitchener was booming. The city's business development office worked to attract more businesses. Proximity to Toronto made the city an increasingly attractive place for homes and businesses. In 1986 residential construction was up by 58 percent. Along with a continuing emphasis on improved services, the city embarked upon several streetscape programs to rejuvenate the King Street business district, and in 1988 a new urban/interurban transit terminal was opened on Charles Street.

Kitchener has indeed come full circle. The administrative centre of the community is being re-established where it first began—on King Street—and the city as a whole is looking to the future with tremendous pride in the accomplishments of the past. Perhaps most striking is the pride taken in the community's German heritage. Although Kitchener is indeed a multi-cultural city, the German heritage remains woven into the cultural fabric. In 1969, only 53 years after anti-German sentiment had forced the community to abandon its name, Kitchener joined with Waterloo in hosting the first annual Oktoberfest celebration. Oktoberfest became Canada's largest Bavarian festival and, just as "Busy Berlin" had done in the early days, the word Oktoberfest has become a symbol of the community, not just in Ontario or across Canada, but throughout all of North America and parts of Europe.

Glass office towers and Victorian hotels—family shops and international retail establishments—sidewalk sales and bicycle races. That's Downtown Kitchener—a place where you can feel the heartbeat of the city.

Yet, with all its big city amenities, Kitchener has retained an attractive small-town feel. It has the best of both worlds—a unique blend of new and old which gives Kitchener a distinctive character and a charm all its own. Many people regard it as a special place in which to live or do business, a feeling that seems to have prevailed for many years.

Like other cities of similar size, Kitchener has not matured as a prosperous and competitive city without experiencing growing pains. Most often these tensions have been reflected in the downtown core, the most visible and sensitive section of the city. In coping with rapid growth and considerable change, civic leaders have devised a number of imaginative plans for future growth. Without question, the most ambitious and exciting project is the construction of

2 LAYING THE CORNERSTONE

Low-rise commercial buildings on King Street surround the significantly taller Canada Trust Building. Photo by Judy-Ann Cazemier/First Light

RIGHT: Oxlea Tower on Frederick Street has housed Kitchener's council chambers and city offices for about 20 years. Photo by Winston Fraser

ABOVE: Depictions of men and women attired in regional costumes of their homelands adorn the Oktoberfest pole, a city landmark. Photo by Glen Jones

a new City Hall and Civic Square on King Street West, in the heart of the downtown shopping and business area. Construction of the new city hall, in the block bounded by King, Young, Duke, and College streets, will involve the removal of the last remaining downtown supermarket, Dutch Boy, as well as several other well-known retail outlets. By the summer of 1993, when the new complex is scheduled to be completed, the look and character of downtown Kitchener will have changed dramatically.

In 1989, when plans for this project were an-

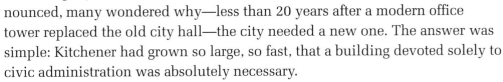

nounced, many wondered why—less than 20 years after a modern office tower replaced the old city hall—the city needed a new one. The answer was simple: Kitchener had grown so large, so fast, that a building devoted solely to civic administration was absolutely necessary.

In its notice inviting architects from across Canada to enter a national design competition, the city noted that the decision to build a new city hall followed "a period of consistent growth during which the current leased facility has become inadequate not only in its size but also in its ability to accommodate public activities and to symbolize the aspirations of the community." The ultimate goal of the project was to create a focal point for the downtown, a long-term administrative centre reflecting the city's rich traditions.

Clearly, the cultural implications of such an endeavour carried a great deal of weight, since the new building was expected to set an architectural mood for future developments. The city was explicit in its instructions that any designs submitted

should be appropriate to the scale and character of the downtown while anticipating and leading redevelopment in the vicinity. They should be dignified without being intimidating, open, accessible to all, inviting and easy to use. They should reflect the values of this vibrant community with its multi-cultural roots, industrious and progressive economy, stability, friendliness, pride in the past and confidence in the future.

The winning design, by Kuwabara, Payne, McKenna, Blumberg of Toronto, features an interior square adjacent to an exterior square so the building can accommodate major public functions all year round. The new council chambers will hold up to 200 citizens. A day-care centre will serve city employees and other downtown employees. The building encompasses 215,000 square feet and a 500-car parking garage will ease parking congestion. It is estimated that the new building will meet city staffing needs until the year 2008, when projections indicate there will be 432 city employees. To draw people from King Street, space is being provided for shops and a restaurant. The total cost of the project is $68,213,000.

The project has met with wide approval. Architecture critic Adele Freedman wrote in the *Toronto Globe & Mail,* "The scheme is notable for its transparency, energy and graceful sweep . . . The City of Kitchener must be congratulated on taking the route it did." The *Toronto Star*'s Christopher Hume had this to say:

Kitchener's new civic centre is three years from completion, but already it has changed the image of the city. The design . . . is a standout. But more important, it was chosen through an open National Competition . . . By going the competition route, City of Kitchener officials made it clear that they were as committed to excellence as they were open to new ideas.

Val Rynnimeri of the University of Waterloo's School of Architecture summed it up best in the *Kitchener-Waterloo Record*: "I am going to give my overall opinion now: Build it!"

Ambitious plans for Kitchener's downtown core are not new. In fact, the history of the community is dotted with plans of equally wide scope and importance—impressive plans which, more often than not, were simply outpaced by the astonishingly rapid growth of the city. Even the gloomiest of doomsayers could not have predicted that, less than two decades after the old

city hall was torn down, rented quarters in the Oxlea Tower would prove inadequate. The proposed City Hall and Civic Square has been a far less contentious issue than the 1973 construction of Market Square. This fact illustrates how the people of Kitchener have come to accept the growth of their community, and indicates how their energy and industry have found a focus in the belief that a major centre like Kitchener needs a vibrant core area in order to maintain a high level of prosperity.

During the past two decades many developments in Kitchener have pointed to a "coming of age," a maturity based upon a conscious return to the values that made Berlin the leading community between Toronto and London in the early days of the twentieth century. In many ways, the planning of a city hall and civic square on King Street represents the closing of a long and historic circle that had its beginning well over 150 years ago—only a few blocks from where the transplanted "heart of the city" will be located.

Religion has played an important part in the expansion and growth of the downtown. The centre of the community was viewed as a practical location for churches. But not every religious group choosing to locate downtown could be considered part of Berlin's religious mainstream.

Jacob Stroh, reminiscing about King Street in the 1840s, recalled that a religious group called the Millerites occupied a small building on the main thoroughfare. Preaching fire and brimstone, the members believed that the world would come to a cataclysmic end in 1844. Seeing the need for some levity in the face of the Millerite's apocalyptic fervor, newspaper publisher Henry Eby, the bishop's son, noted in the *Duetsche Canadier;* "Inasmuch as the end of the world is to come on March 22, according to Miller's prophecy, we respectfully request all our readers who are in arrears with their subscriptions to call and settle at once—otherwise it will go hard with them on Judgement Day." Although the community was founded on Christian principles and the settlers generally lived their lives as the Bible taught, the Millerites were such an aberration that even devout Mennonites like Eby found it difficult to avoid comment. Speaker's Corner at the intersection of King and Benton streets is perhaps a modern reflection of the tolerance accorded the Millerites. The freedom to express different opinions has remained a cherished and well-used right in Kitchener.

Most of the denominations who found a home in Berlin first located in the downtown area. Between 1813 and the late 1850s, the Mennonites, Lutherans,

Swedenborgians, Roman Catholics, Methodists, Evangelicals, Presbyterians, and Anglicans established congregations and built churches in the downtown core. Many of these congregations, while greatly expanded from the early years, are still located downtown, the church spires calling to mind an era when the social life of the community revolved around the churches. It may even be said that the presence of so many major congregations helped to anchor the neighbourhoods which became such a feature of the core area.

Today the old neighbourhoods are seen as a valuable heritage resource, and every effort—from zoning to heritage designation—is made to ensure that they remain a vital part of the downtown. The churches made the downtown core a hub of social activity long after it had become a commercial area. They are still responsible for attracting worshippers from the farthest reaches of Forest Heights or Stanley Park to the downtown each Sunday.

Berlin's selection as the county seat in 1852, its incorporation as a village in 1854, and the arrival of the Grand Trunk Railway in 1856 created a boom in the community that saw Berlin's business district replace the downtown core of neighbouring Galt as the leading commercial centre in Waterloo County. Ironically, it was not a Berliner at all, but Sheriff George Grange of Guelph who was primarily responsible for shaping the urban landscape of the downtown's western end after the arrival of the railway. Benefiting from an insider's knowledge

ABOVE: The simple, small-scale architecture of Waterloo Township Hall contrasts greatly with the grand, 215,000-square-foot proposed city hall and civic square. Photo by Winston Fraser

of the proposed route, he purchased and surveyed a large tract of land along the railway, hoping to sell the lots for homes. When the buyers never materialized, Grange found himself with some rather substantial and entirely unexpected financial difficulties. As a consequence larger lots were sold as factory sites. Thus, heavy industry was drawn to that end of the downtown, leaving the bulk of King Street to shopkeepers and suppliers of various services. The Epton and Kaufman Footwear plants on King Street at the western end of the downtown core remain as evidence of that era. In the intervening years, the houses, churches, and small manufacturing concerns on King Street were gradually replaced by commercial and retail establishments. The seat of local government was first established at Frederick and King streets and has remained there since. Thus, the main street of downtown Kitchener has long been characterized by a business-commercial centre anchored at opposite ends by manufacturing and local government. It is quite significant that construction of the new City Hall and Civic Square near the western end of the city's core will mark a major departure from this downtown dichotomy. Such developments are proof positive that Kitchenerites, while conscious and proud of civic traditions, understand that a vital and thriving downtown cannot survive on tradition alone. It is typical of Kitchener that a middle ground was sought and agreed upon.

The various city halls in Kitchener's history have by no means been the only landmarks of note in the downtown. By the 1870s the Saturday Farmers' Market had become a local fixture. Although cattle fairs had been popular in the area since the 1830s, the idea for a farmers' market was not advanced until Jacob Y. Shantz suggested in 1859 that Berlin combine a cattle fair with a produce market. Despite the initial reluctance of several leading citizens, such a fair was held, and the idea quickly grew so popular that by 1866 the village had begun to discuss building a permanent market building. In 1869 Shantz built the first market building. So began a tradition that, in the intervening 120 years, has become one of the most popular tourist attractions in the Region of Waterloo.

Expanding quickly, the market had outgrown the original building by 1907, and was replaced by a much larger structure in a prominent location beside the city hall on Frederick Street. As late as the 1950s it was said that a person returning to Kitchener after an absence of decades would feel right at home after only a few seconds inside the market.

The market building was demolished in 1973 during construction of the aptly named Market Square shopping centre. Many sentimental Kitchenerites purchased the familiar red bricks from the old market as souvenirs. Today the Kitchener Farmers' Market retains much of the charm and old-fashioned values that Jacob Y. Shantz had envisioned and would immediately recognize. The *Toronto Star* summed up the enduring attractiveness of Kitchener's market in a 1989 article: "It's a people place where the ambience is Old World European blended with Early Rural Canadian."

Visitors to Kitchener from around the world make a stop at the market a must. There they meet merchants whose families have worked the market for over a century. They can stroll between aisles of fresh meats, produce, cheeses, pastries, and a wide variety of local crafts. If they're careful, they may hear the rare sounds of the Pennsylvania-German dialect being spoken. Old-timers are always delighted when a visitor from Pennsylvania stops by and joins in the conversation.

Yet another landmark, Victoria Park (which has figured prominently in several plans for the revitalization of Kitchener's downtown), was almost never purchased for public use. Ironically, those opposed to the acquisition based their objections on the fact that the park was too far out of town. When plans were announced for a man-made lake, residents complained that the water would stagnate. Cartoons showing a cow drinking the lake dry were posted in several downtown windows. More often than not, a calm discussion about the merits of a public park degenerated into a heated shouting match. But the pro-

The landmark Walper Terrace Hotel, named for Currie Walper (the original owner), is a testament to elegance, hospitality, and service. Photo by Judy-Ann Cazemier/First Light

ponents eventually had their way.

Soon after the park opened in 1896 a strip of land was purchased, allowing Courtland Avenue to be extended from Queen Street to the park entrance. The road through the park completed a link with Park Street and provided another route to Waterloo. It remains today one of the most well-travelled sections of road in the city. The original boat house and pavilion were destroyed in a spectacular 1916 fire. The smoke and flames attracted a huge crowd. By then there was no question how important the park had become to the community.

In fact, the park was the sports focus for the city for half a century. A stadium, built on the site of a sports field which pre-dated the park itself, had mobile walls that could be moved to form either a baseball diamond or football field. The construction of Centennial Stadium and Jack Couch Baseball Park in the late 1960s marked the end of Victoria Park as a major sports venue. Nevertheless, it remains a popular place to spend leisure time.

Besides the many stirring athletic contests, the park was also the scene of one of the most famous incidents in the history of the community. In 1897 a group of citizens erected a bust of Germany's Kaiser Wilhelm I in the park to commemorate the community's German heritage. In 1909 the Imperial Order of the Daughters of the Empire erected a statue of Queen Victoria to commemorate the bonds between Germany and England. While the bust of the Kaiser was tossed into the park lake during World War I, vanishing forever, the statue of Queen Victoria still stands watch over pleasure boaters, picnickers, athletes, and a wide variety of other park patrons.

The baseball bleachers and light standards are gone now, but a decorative fountain graces the once-ridiculed lake, the surrounding woods provide a safe home for a variety of waterfowl and wildlife, and the latest pavilion serves a variety of community activities. As for being too far out of town, Victoria Park has become as much a part of the downtown scene as King Street itself. In fact, some felt that the proposed city hall should be built on the site of adjacent Victoria School—incorporating the old building in the design for the new one. In many ways the existence of the park, and the important role it continues to play in the daily life of Kitchener, is a tribute to those with the vision to see how the community would grow. This vision is evident in Kitchener's ongoing efforts to enhance the image of the downtown core.

Of course, no community grows to the levels of prosperity attained by Kitchener without a broad network of financial institutions. It is hardly surprising that Berlin's rise as a formidable commercial centre was accompanied by the opening of banks in the downtown area. Similarly, it is not surprising that Berliners played key roles in the founding of several important insurance companies, including those in Waterloo. Despite Berlin's involvement in financial matters, it is quite telling that Waterloo became known as the "Hartford of Canada" in recognition of its many insurance companies while Berlin/Kitchener was linked to such American manufacturing centres as Grand Rapids, Michigan (furniture), and Akron, Ohio (rubber). The implications were obvious. Kitchener was where things got done. And downtown was where the action was.

The Hersel Haus and Fiedler's Deli offer tasty dining fare to Kitchener residents and visitors. Photo by Judy-Ann Cazemier/First Light

Berlin's first financial institution, a branch of the Bank of Upper Canada, was opened on Queen Street North in 1853, one year after Berlin was named the county seat. This branch was replaced by the Commercial Bank in 1860. The Merchants Bank assumed control in 1868 and was absorbed by the Bank of Montreal in 1922. The Canadian Bank of Commerce opened a branch on King Street in 1879, followed by the Bank of Hamilton in 1893. The Bank of Nova Scotia occupied space in the Canadian Block in 1900, and the Bank of Toronto (1906), Dominion Bank (1907), Royal Bank of Canada (1919), and Imperial Bank of Canada (1926) also located in the core area.

Today the names have changed, but the number of downtown banks remains high. The Canadian Imperial Bank of Commerce occupies a beautifully restored building across Queen Street from the landmark Walper Terrace Hotel. The National Bank is located in the stately and carefully restored former Public Utilities Commission headquarters at King and Gaukel streets. Also downtown are the Bank of Montreal, Lloyds Bank of Canada, the Bank of Nova Scotia, and the Toronto Dominion Bank, which began replacing one downtown branch with a modern office complex in the summer of 1990. The Royal Bank is located in the Corporation Square building on Duke Street. Trust companies, including Canada Trust, Royal Trust, Montreal Trust, and National Trust, maintain offices in the heart of Kitchener. They all have one thing in common—a strong belief in the downtown as a profitable commercial centre with a long and successful history of making things happen.

In 1991 Canada Trust and its real estate development arm, Truscan Realty,

The Kitchener Public Library provides residents with volumes of educational and entertaining literature. Photo by Judy-Ann Cazemier/First Light

started another chapter to the evolution of Kitchener's core when it began construction of a 12-storey, double-towered, 296,000-square-foot office building at the corner of King and Ontario streets. With a projected cost of $45 million, the ultra-modern building will feature a central atrium and will be clad in granite and glass. Architects were careful in designing the structure to fit the context of King Street—making sure that the tower doesn't cast the obtrusive shadows so common in other urban centres. When demolition of the old building began in the fall of 1990, the original architecture was slowly revealed as the stone cladding was removed. Old painted signs and ornate brickwork, hidden for decades, again saw the light of day. Pedestrians along King Street stopped to watch, surprised by what had been there in years gone by. The decades-old art deco style Medical Arts Building was also removed to accommodate the new tower.

If the original 12-storey Waterloo Trust and Savings Co. (Canada Trust) building at King and Water streets changed the look of the downtown area when it was built in 1961, the new structure can be expected to accomplish that and more. After all, Waterloo Trust, a local institution founded by businesspeople from both Kitchener and Waterloo, has roots reaching deep into the community, and the company has been prominent in many different efforts to enhance the reputation of the "Twin Cities."

As the downtown core is refurbished and modernized, Kitchener's first-rate transit system will be counted upon more than ever to quickly and efficiently move the shoppers, businesspeople, and other commuters to and from the core area. Kitchener Transit, 100 years old in 1989, provides a vital link with the growing suburbs. The Berlin and Waterloo Street Railway ushered in the era of public transportation in 1889 when it began operating a daily schedule between Berlin and Waterloo using horse-drawn streetcars. One car left each end of the route every hour on the hour—12 hours a day. Sleighs were used during the winter months. In 1895 the use of horses was discontinued in favour of electric trolleys, a technological marvel at the time. Power was derived from the Breithaupt family's electric plant. The Town of Berlin assumed control of the

line in 1906 and turned its operation over to the Public Utilities Commission.

Crosstown bus service began in 1939, with a fleet of five bright yellow electric trolley coaches heralding the end of the streetcars. Overhead lines were installed for the coaches in 1946, replacing the old familiar side lines and adding a new dimension to the look of the downtown. Diesel-powered coaches were added to the system in Canada's centennial year and the old trolleys were gradually phased out, the last one removed from service in 1973. That same year the City of Kitchener took control of the system from the Public Utilities Commission and Kitchener Transit was born. A transit terminal, part of a downtown revitalization scheme, was opened on Duke Street across from the new Market Square complex in 1974. Since that time the "Get Around Gang" (an advertising slogan used by Kitchener Transit) has added a computerized Teleride system, advising commuters when a vehicle is expected to arrive at a specific stop. All vehicles are also equipped with two-way radios, a necessary tool for a transportation system covering 15 routes and 18,200 kilometres daily.

When the system outgrew its Duke Street terminal, the City of Kitchener gave a major boost to downtown revitalization by building a $9-million urban/interurban transit terminal on Charles Street, one arm of the downtown "ring road" encircling King Street. As with the new city hall, construction of the transit terminal meant the demolition of an entire city block, dramatically altering the look of the downtown. Like Canada Trust, Kitchener Transit is making a major contribution to keeping the downtown a vibrant and exciting place.

The current revitalization of Kitchener's core area promises to add a group of significant new structures—buildings which will help replace many landmarks lost to

The Centre in the Square is evidence of the continuing growth of downtown Kitchener. Photo by Winston Fraser

Kitchener Transit is contributing to the rebirth and revitalization of downtown with its 15 routes and 18,200 kilometers travelled daily. Photo by Dave Prichard/ First Light

time. This process of replacement has happened throughout the history of the city, but has been most notable when structures like the venerable Dunker Building are demolished—in this case to make way for the King Centre shopping complex. Built in 1929, the seven-storey Dunker Building was Kitchener's first "skyscraper." The mall replacing it, directly across King Street from the city hall site, has since been renamed the King Value Centre and houses major discount retail outlets run by both Sears and Robinsons.

Other familiar downtown landmarks now gone include the Kitchener Firehall on Frederick Street. Located opposite the old city hall, it was demolished in 1960. The Kaufman Lumber Company, built west of the railway tracks when the property was considered too far from the downtown to succeed, was soon overtaken by urban expansion and less than a decade ago was replaced by a retail and convenience mall. A brewery which stood for many years on Victoria Street opposite the Kaufman Footwear plant was replaced by a doughnut shop.

One could scarcely have grown up in Kitchener and not been familiar with the names Goudie and Walper. The Goudie name was made famous by A.R. Goudie, who in 1909 established a dry-goods business with his father-in-law, Arthur Weseloh. By 1934 the business had become the community's leading department store. The store had more than 30 departments occupying more than 100,000 square feet of space on several floors. It was a rare individual who did not own something purchased at Goudies, and the 180-seat Grill Room restaurant was a favorite meeting place for downtown shoppers and employees alike. More than one business deal was cemented over lunch there. When Goudie died in 1960, his son Stuart assumed control of the business. It was scaled down in the 1980s and eventually closed. Part of the building was converted into a street-level mall. In 1989 plans were announced for a complete renovation of the premises and a return to retail shopping.

The Walper name was made famous by C.H. "Curry" Walper, who built the present Walper Terrace Hotel on the site of his devastated Commercial Hotel in 1892. The Commercial had been destroyed in a spectacular fire several months earlier. Before beginning construction, Walper offered to sell Berlin Council the adjacent 14-foot strip of land, which caused a peculiar jog in Queen Street where it crossed King Street. Council initially accepted the $500 price, but the people of Berlin howled at the extravagance of their representatives and the councillors reversed their decision. The matter was quickly dropped and the jog in the road at King and Queen Streets, while bewildering to visitors, has become a rather quaint reminder to Kitchenerites of how the past has shaped the present and, indeed, how everything done in the present has the potential to shape the future. But not all observers appreciate how such things add to Kitchener's charm. In 1967 a local newspaper reporter complained that because the strange corner was allowed to remain "three generations have worn out shoe leather walking the extra steps."

The reporter's frustration with the amount of effort needed to navigate the

Hundreds of Kitchener residents will occupy this huge apartment complex (shown under construction) near Mill Park Drive. Photo by Winston Fraser

Walper corner likely stems from the fact that until 1973 the *K-W Record* was a downtown business itself. The newspaper has functioned under a variety of names since 1878, when it was founded as the *Daily News.* It has also been known as the *Berlin Daily Record, Berlin News Record, The News Record, The Daily Record, Kitchener Daily Record,* and *Kitchener-Waterloo Record.* When the newspaper moved to a new headquarters on Fairway Road, it marked the first time in the city's history that the community newspaper was not based downtown.

Today Kitchener is continuing a process of urban renewal begun in the 1960s. Streetscape projects have been given an added impetus through the efforts of downtown businesspeople who have chosen to refurbish the Victorian and Edwardian facades of their properties. As a result of their efforts, King Street has remained an attractive spot for community events ranging from summer carnivals to major bicycle races and the ever-popular Oktoberfest and Santa Claus parades. The Kitchener Downtown Business Association is an active supporter and promoter of downtown revitalization. Organized in 1977, the KDBA is administered by a volunteer board of directors including representatives from city council. Several committees (marketing, parking, municipal affairs, and street beautification) occupy about 50 volunteer staff members. The marketing committee develops and implements advertising and promotional campaigns. Street decorations—including seasonal street banners, decorative lights on trees, and Christmas decorations—are purchased by the street beautification group. The municipal affairs and parking committees deal with civic administrators on matters of concern to downtown businesses such as the availability of parking, policing, and general upkeep.

As Kitchener steps boldly into the last decade of the twentieth century, there can be little doubt that the city's core area will continue to play a vital role in future development. Although a number of imaginative and modern buildings are currently in the works, many older structures remain. The combination of buildings reflect different eras—each one a symbol of the drive and determination which made Kitchener an important Canadian city. Whether bathed in the summer sun or covered in a blanket of fresh snow, the pulse of Kitchener continues to course through the downtown streets—common ground for the old and the new.

The *Toronto Globe* reporter was unequivocal in his praise of the thriving community:

It is in the evening . . . after the bells have tolled the summons to cease work, that the extent of the industry of Berlin is made evident. Along King Street and down Queen come throngs of work people from the factories, laughing, joking, cheerful and contented. There are many women workers too, not the pale, undeveloped girls of city workshops, but bright, plump, ruddy-faced lasses, who do not feel life is a burden and work an unending weariness. There are two sides to the making of wealth. Men do not say, looking at Pittsburgh, "Pittsburgh is becoming rich," they say, "Carnegie is making millions." There is nothing of that in Berlin.

Berlin in 1889 was, without question, "the most rapidly expanding and liveliest town west of Toronto." Many years after Berlin became Kitchener, the same holds true. A healthy diversity of industry has allowed a collective prosperity to continue.

3 MAKING A GOOD THING BETTER

A bounty of fresh tomatoes makes its colourful contribution to the Farmer's Market.
Photo by Glen Jones

Today Kitchener is the best location for business in North America. Situated on the Macdonald-Cartier Freeway (Highway 401), it is less than one hour from booming Metropolitan Toronto and the rapidly expanding Lester B. Pearson International Airport. It is just over two hours from the U.S. border at Windsor and the automobile manufacturers in and around Detroit. Similarly, Buffalo, New York, is two hours away, and access to the St. Lawrence Seaway system is available either through the Port of Hamilton 30 miles away or several smaller Lake Huron ports. As a Chamber of Commerce publication recently put it, "From here, anywhere is near."

As a business location, Kitchener has established an enviable reputation. With a wide diversity of industry and an advanced network of services, the city is poised to embark upon a second century of growth and prosperity. One key to the future lies in Kitchener's hospitable climate. Located in southwestern Ontario, Kitchener has established a profitable mix of agriculture, industry, and commerce. Food processing giant J.M. Schneider, Inc., has grown to become the area's largest employer, and scores of bountiful family farms are but a few minute's drive from the downtown core. A short distance away, Canada's most respected agricultural university—the University of Guelph—maintains a position on the cutting edge of research and development.

Although early Berlin depended upon a strong agricultural base for its economic well-being, it soon became clear that, unlike many other Ontario communities, it was not a traditional market town. During the first decades of settlement, the inhabitants had little choice but to trade with one another as a means of survival. But as the ability of individuals to fend for themselves began to develop, so too did an entrepreneurial spirit that became the community's signature. While agriculture remained important, people came to the realization that there were other ways to prosper. They built factories, stores, hotels, and shops. Word of their industriousness spread far beyond the bounds of the community, and their products became a part of everyday life for miles around. Agriculture was not abandoned for something better. It merely became a part of

Kitchener is home to a thriving commercial and retail community. Photo by Glen Jones

a broad economic synthesis that would see the community become a leading commercial centre, replete with many of the services found lacking in other larger cities.

Kitchener people are proud of the fact that no single industry has dominated the local economy. In the early years diversity was largely the result of the varied skills brought to the community by immigrant Germans. Furniture makers like Jacob Hailer, John Hoffman, Adam Klippert, John Anthes, Noah Ziegler, Daniel Hibner, and Hartman Krug did not come to Berlin because it was famous for its furniture—they came because the people spoke their language. But in time their skills and energy made Berlin famous for its fine furniture. The town became known as the "Grand Rapids of Canada," in tribute to America's foremost centre of furniture production. Similarly, Reinhold Lang and Louis Breithaupt did not settle in Berlin because of its famous leather industry. On the contrary, they started it and made it famous. But, like the furniture industry, the leather industry augmented rather than dominated the local economy.

Perhaps the rise and fall of the button industry is most indicative of the importance of industrial diversity. For a time, Berlin/Kitchener was the undisputed "Button Capital of Canada." Indeed, when Jacob Y. Shantz, John J. Woelfle, and a talented artisan named Emil Vogelsang established the Dominion Button Works in 1870, it became only the second such enterprise in North America—the other being located near Rochester, New York. Vogelsang quit to establish his own business several years later, and Shantz carried on. The plant was twice destroyed by fire, in 1899 and 1910. At the time of the second fire, the firm was the largest employer in Berlin. Such a disaster could well have dealt an overly dependent economy a mortal blow, but the town's diversified industrial foundation cushioned the impact. Later, when American competition put other button firms out of business, a plethora of other industries were there

Kitchener, as evidenced by its strong, modern architecture, has become a leading commercial centre. Photo by Winston Fraser

While many of Kitchener's businesses have been absorbed by national corporations, Kaufman Footwear Ltd. has remained a local company. Photo by Judy-Ann Cazemier/First Light

to take up the slack. From the very beginning, Kitchener has remained aloof from the boom-and-bust cycles that regularly torment "one industry" centres. That makes the city a very stable place in which to invest and do business.

A look at a cross-section of Kitchener's largest industries illustrates how diverse the economy has remained over the years while at the same time showing how well traditional industries like rubber and food products have adapted to changing times. Among the leading businesses are Schneider Corporation (processed foods), Electrohome Limited (communications and electronics), Kaufman Footwear (boots and shoes), MTD Products (lawn and garden equipment), Epton Industries (rubber and plastics), Dare Foods (biscuits and candies), and Uniroyal-Goodrich (tires, rubber, and plastic products). Each one has carved out a significant niche, not just in the local economy, but provincially and nationally as well. Some are becoming more well known in the United States, Europe, and Pacific Rim countries like Japan and Korea. Where once the

"Made in Berlin" label had been the community's rallying cry, now the phrase "Made in Kitchener" is gaining wide acceptance as being synonymous with high quality.

Other successful businesses call Kitchener home as well. Budd Canada is one of North America's leading suppliers of automobile frames, and Lear Seigler makes numerous car seat components. Ball Brothers Limited is a long-established general contractor, well known throughout Ontario. Boehmers supplies heating fuel and concrete products over a wide area. Canadian Blower/Canada Pumps (pumps and boiler components), Chicopee Manufacturing (aerospace components), John Forsyth Ltd. (clothing), The Arrow Company (clothing), and The Prudential Assurance Company (property and casualty insurance) are but a few of the large and successful companies operating in the community. Their success has brought wide acclaim to Kitchener.

The notion that local products are unsurpassed in quality is not an old one. In fact, the people of Berlin once staged a Made-in-Berlin exhibition to display the proud community's products. Ontario Premier Sir James P. Whitney, who officially opened the 12-day extravaganza, proclaimed, "Today Berlin stands at the head of the procession in the Dominion. I will tell people to come here for lessons in enterprise and progress." So successful was the occasion that a similar exhibition was held in conjunction with Berlin's 1912 "Celebration of Cityhood."

Among the products exhibited were ladies' garments from the Star Whitewear Co., biscuits and confectionery from C. Doerr & Co., cooking utensils made at the Berlin Aluminum Works, and "racycles," a type of bicycle manufactured by Arthur Pequegnat in a small shop on Frederick Street. J.M. Schneider's famous sausages were featured, as were furniture made by Hartman Krug and leather products manufactured by the Lang and Breithaupt families.

The **Kitchener-Waterloo Record** *building houses the operations of the descendant of Kitchener's first daily newspaper.* **Photo by Winston Fraser**

Kitchener's varied and expansive industrial tapestry was woven with the encouragement of civic officials, who spent a great deal of effort to assure a profitable future for the community. From the introduction of a factory policy and the institution of tax incentives and bonuses in the late nineteenth century to pioneering efforts in the field of urban planning in the 1920s, Kitchener

Many structures were removed to make way for the Market Square complex. The building stands on land once occupied by the old city hall, Farmer's Market, rows of stores, and a bakery. Photo by Glen Jones

has always shown a desire to facilitate better tomorrows through work in the present.

Kitchener's attention to industrial planning was primarily responsible for generating the impressive growth of the 1960s and 1970s. In the early 1960s planning commissioner William E. Thomson recognized the wave of the future by detailing the need for an improved and more structured approach to growth. In his mind, the solution lay in some type of regional government. Others shared his concerns, and in 1970 a review was conducted of the overlapping and confusing structure of local and county government. In 1973 the Ontario government created the Regional Municipality of Waterloo, which brought together three cities and four townships to work in concert for the benefit of the area as a whole. While industrial development remained under local jurisdiction, it has benefited from a regional approach to land use planning, and in many ways individual municipalities have shared in the growth that has occurred since the regional municipality was created.

The most evident feature of industrial change in Kitchener since World War II—causing a complete rethinking of industrial planning—has been the dispersal of industry from the core area. There was simply not enough land available for the major expansions undertaken by local businesses. The demands of the modern-day marketplace replaced many long-held beliefs about the role and location of large factories. Gone were the days when local firms operated in the city centre close to the homes of the workers. Second- and third-generation suc-

cessors to the pioneers who established many of Berlin's major businesses had
to replace older buildings and machinery with up-to-date plants, where productivity and efficiency were key ingredients. Kaufman Footwear and B.F.
Goodrich were only two examples of old established businesses which
expanded by creating factories on sites removed from the downtown area.

In many ways 1965 was a turning point for industrial planning in Kitchener.
That year the booming city became the fastest growing community in Canada,
outpacing economic and urban growth in many larger centres like Calgary and
Vancouver in the west and Montreal in the east. But unlike other communities,
Kitchener remained conscious that, although it was desirable to have several

ABOVE AND RIGHT:
One of the advantages of
a strong agricultural
heritage is the availabil-
ity of seasonal fruit at a
variety of convenient
locations. Above photo by
Glen Jones; right photo by
Dave Prichard/First Light

dominant industries in the area, true growth was represented by the presence of a wide variety of different businesses.

The Chamber of Commerce has played a key role in creating an industrial mixture characterized by an unbounded energy and vitality. Although the chamber has actively promoted industrial growth since its early days as the Board of Trade, it was not until the late 1950s that its involvement was institutionalized.

In 1958 the City of Kitchener formally handed over to the chamber the responsibility for industrial development. At the time many leading businessmen were convinced that such development was so important to the progress of the community that only the chamber had the expertise to properly organize and undertake a program to attract more businesses to Kitchener. In retrospect, the move was a fortunate one. Between 1958 and 1960 the chamber attracted 18 new industries to Kitchener. The expansionist atmosphere also resulted in 25 existing industries building 29 additions. The city administration proved a willing and co-operative partner. Freed of the task of marketing the community, the city was able to concentrate on projects ranging from revitalization of the core area to an expansion of the social services necessitated by the increase in industrial activity.

Responding to the challenge, the chamber formed a business development committee under the direction of assistant manager Kenneth Burke. According to a published history of the chamber, "the move would facilitate greater access and a better working relationship with other civic employees such as the city engineer, assessor, planner, solicitor, land purchaser and treasurer." Of course, such inter-relationships made perfect sense and, while hardly revolutionary, served to stimulate a new attitude in the city. Clearly there was merit in planning Kitchener's future prosperity, rather than simply letting the marketplace dictate the directions taken. Today Kitchener commands the respect of other communities for its early recognition of the merits inherent in the co-operation between business and government. While other communities

A Waterloo Metal Stamping Company truck makes its way through Kitchener. Photo by Winston Fraser

were only beginning such relationships, Kitchener was consolidating the gains already made.

Much of Kitchener's present industrial philosophy was shaped by the chamber during the rapid growth of the 1960s and 1970s. Perhaps the most important occurrence during the chamber's role as chief promoter of Kitchener's industrial interests was construction of a $7-million tire plant south of Fairway Road by B.F. Goodrich Canada Ltd.

Long one of Kitchener's leading businesses, the company had operated since the 1930s at the corner of King and Victoria streets, across from the Kaufman Footwear plant. When it found itself out of space, the company announced that sites outside of Kitchener were being considered. Chamber members complained loudly that Goodrich was leaving because the city had no attractive land left for industrial development.

A recent study by the University of Waterloo's Department of Geography concluded that the "move by Goodrich sparked off the city's industrial park phase." Led by Ira G. Needles—an influential member of the chamber and an staunch advocate of industrial planning—Goodrich obtained a 100-acre, fully serviced site for $1,000 per acre near the intersection of Fairway Road and Wilson Avenue. Most observers heaved a huge sigh of relief when Goodrich decided to stay. Needles had advanced the chamber's cause immeasurably, making his point about the lack of industrial land in the clearest of terms. The Goodrich plant was expanded twice before 1968, and, according to University of Waterloo researchers, "the area around it quickly became one of rapid industrial growth" —dramatically driving home the point Needles had been making for years.

As a result of the Goodrich move, 200 acres of adjacent land were assembled and zoned as an industrial park. The Goodrich plant attracted other businesses, and it was soon apparent that the industrial park was a smashing success. This prompted the city to assemble an additional 305 acres in the same area, and in less than a year more than one-third of the cost had been recovered through sales. The tone of economic development had been set for generations to come.

The efforts of the chamber and the civic administration soon began to pay dividends. Employment levels rose and the city's already diverse economic base became more diversified. The city's Business Development Department summed it up with a slogan: "Kitchener, The Good Life."

The relationship between business and government came full circle in the 1980s when the City of Kitchener assumed full control of economic development from the chamber. It was felt that the civic administration and the chamber were duplicating efforts where they could be consolidated to become more effective. A Business Development Department was placed under the control of William E. Thomson, former city (later regional) planning commissioner, and charged with the task of promoting economic growth. Chamber members—business and professional people with a broad range of experience and expertise—continue to give their time as members of an advisory committee reinforcing the work of the Business Development Department.

Kitchener is taking a very pro-active approach to success in the 1990s. Thomson envisions an ever-expanding diversity of businesses in the community. "I haven't discovered any major weaknesses," he says. "But there are some holes—in the pharmaceutical industry and the whole industry catering to the aged. We're targeting to bring them here."

In addition, there will be an increase in the amount and level of job training available. Says Jack Middlemass, general manager of the chamber, "When I started working in the mid '50s, the philosophy was to look at advancing through the same company for 45 years. Today it's different. The technology is out there; it is coming at us much faster. The employer must start budgeting money to keep pace with retraining needs." Ideas like this will work to keep Kitchener energized and competitive.

Today the Kitchener Chamber of Commerce is comprised of 1,000 member firms and over 1,400 delegates. Their collective aim is simple: To promote the civic, economic, and social welfare of Kitchener. Besides its business activities, the chamber also oversees the Visitor and Convention Bureau, which has been very successful in promoting Kitchener as a tourist destination. The chamber

The King Value Center is proof that retail activity is alive and well in Kitchener. Photo by Judy-Ann Cazemier/First Light

also takes an active role in lobbying government and played a major role in the local debate over free trade with the U.S.

The electronics and communications industry—perhaps the largest of the new wave of industries—was primarily responsible for the spectacular rise in the percentage of experienced workers as the number of employees engaged in high-tech industries has more than doubled in the last 25 years. Taking the lead was Carl Pollock's Dominion Electrohome Industries Ltd. When the company celebrated its 50th anniversary in 1957, it employed 1,050 employees in five plants. By 1965 that total had risen to 1,750 employees in nine plants. If anything, the Electrohome experience indicated that Kitchener was an ideal location for high-tech businesses. Pollock's influence as a founder of the University of Waterloo sent a signal to other high-tech manufacturers that Kitchener was moving forward with the times. From day one there has been a constructive link between the research facilities at the university and Kitchener's electronics industry.

Today companies like Automated Tooling Systems have set industry standards for fully integrated robotics and microprocessors. But the innovations have not been limited to manufacturing robots and computers. Kitchener businesses have introduced many imaginative techniques into the workplace. Hostess Foods, for example, has received national recognition for its "Quality Circles" program, which increased worker participation in the running of the company. Companies like Budd Canada have adopted "Statistical Process Control," whereby responsibility for product quality is placed in the hands of the workers. The "Just in Time" approach, which increases management control of production by slashing inventories, has been implemented by other companies. Together, these initiatives will ensure better products, less waste, and more successful Kitchener businesses.

While there is much to be said of the new in Kitchener, the community

Kitchener's healthy commercial and manufacturing base has benefited from the leadership of its civic and financial bodies. This is the Royal Bank Building. Photo by Dave Prichard/First Light

would be substantially less successful were it not for the leadership of its established companies. A prime example is Electrohome.

Although a local fixture for decades, Electrohome has been in the vanguard of the city's progressive industries. Of great significance was the role the firm played in the development of Kitchener's industrial parks strategy. In the early 1960s, when Ira Needles was pressuring the city for more industrial land, his good friend Carl Pollock, seeking to move Electrohome's headquarters out of the downtown, purchased a large parcel of land on Wellington Street, across from Woodside National Historic Park. At the same time other similarly attractive areas also received industrial zoning, and several large businesses seized the day, expanding into even larger quarters. Significant moves were made by Kaufman Footwear, long a dominating presence in the downtown core, and Ardelt Industries of Canada Limited, a division of West Germany's huge Krupp organization. On the lookout for investment opportunities in Canada, Krupp saw Kitchener as a location brimming with potential. It also didn't hurt that the city was famous for its connection with the fatherland. In a recent study, University of Waterloo Professor David Walker noted how "the main inherent attraction of Kitchener . . . seems to have always been its people. A strong Germanic heritage . . . has been associated with skills, hard work, entrepreneurial activity and good productivity." To use a distinctly 1990s phrase, Krupp could "relate to" Kitchener.

Kaufman moved to an area along the railway tracks near the corner of River Road and Victoria Street (Highway 7), within sight of the large Electrohome plant. The firm still considered it advantageous to be located along a rail line, as it had been for decades. The new plant has attracted many small and medium-sized businesses to adjacent locations, as well as several large shopping plazas. Some nearby companies are quite large, including Spae-Naur Products, Inc., a distributor of mechanical fasteners, and Ball Brothers Ltd., a long-established general contractor.

Ardelt Industries located its new plant on Hansen Avenue, near the Rockway Golf Club and the yet-to-be-constructed Conestoga Parkway. Although it was really the first business to locate in an industrial park setting—the plant was built in 1955—it was not looked upon in that light until it began drawing other companies to the area. The vicinity is now one of Kitchener's major industrial sections, with businesses ranging from Braun Manufacturing, a maker of expansion joints for bridge construction, to Ainsworth Press, a large commercial printer, and Overland Express, a major trucking firm. The close proximity to the Parkway has, as with the Electrohome site, been a tremendous benefit. In Kitchener every effort has been made to locate businesses in areas with the benefit of excellent transportation links.

The automotive industry has been a mainstay of Kitchener's industrial superstructure for decades. Unlike other important industries, however, the automo-

The Kitchener-Waterloo Airport is a busy transportation hub in the area. Photo by Dave Prichard/First Light

bile industry found a comfortable home in Kitchener long after the community had been established as a major industrial centre. Unknown to many is the fact that Kitchener was home to the first production automobiles manufactured in Canada. Produced by Dr. Milton Good and his brother, Nelson, the first automobile assembled by the LeRoy Automobile Company was unveiled in late 1899 or early 1900. The bodies and frames were made of wood by the Kaufman Lumber Company. Their first mass-produced auto, restored by philanthropic meat packer Norman Schneider, is on display at Doon Heritage Crossroads, a re-created pioneer community a short distance from several large auto-related industries.

Also involved in the auto industry was the Redpath Motor Vehicle Company. Based in Hall's Lane, the owners tried to build a replica of a one-cylinder French car, but had little success. At the time, legendary auto maker R.R. Olds was in the area as a guest of Oscar Rumpel—Canada's "Felt King"—and he visited the firm. In Detroit his Oldsmobile company was producing one-cylinder cars with chain drive. But Olds was not convinced that such a vehicle was practical. Having witnessed the futility of Redpath's endeavour, he abandoned his plan and set about making a two-cylinder and, later, a four-cylinder car with shaft drive. Of course, the Oldsmobile became one of the world's most popular cars.

Some believe Olds was not the only automobile pioneer to visit the area around the turn of the century. According to octogenarian insurance man Irvin Erb, Henry Ford came to Berlin around 1900 hoping to obtain enough land and capital to begin production of automobiles. Erb maintains that he got the story straight from the multi-millionaire industrialist himself when the two met in Detroit in 1943. Apparently Ford came to Berlin after hearing about the Good brothers and their attempts at making a reliable "horseless carriage." Unable to interest any local businessmen in his ideas, Ford left Berlin, only to establish what would become one of the world's most important businesses. Ford's adaptation of the assembly line revolutionized North American industry and created a social and environmental revolution unprecedented in world history. Although Ford left Berlin without achieving his goal, it may be argued that Kitchener owes a great deal to the man. By making ownership of an automobile an attainable goal for the average person, Ford ensured that the auto parts industry would grow and prosper. And Kitchener ranks with Windsor and Oshawa as an important centre in Canada's auto industry.

Historians at Ford headquarters in Michigan don't discount Erb's story, but they point out that there is no way of confirming its veracity. They do concede, however, that Ford was frequently in Canada seeking new ideas and searching for capital. The irony of the story is that today Kitchener goes out of its way to lure companies involved in the automobile trade. The economic foundation built since Ford's visit seems almost tailor-made for auto makers. The decision of Japanese automobile giant Toyota to build a massive plant in the hinterland between Kitchener and Cambridge (the plant is actually in Cambridge) offers a clear illustration of how even huge international companies view the area. Planners in both Kitchener and Cambridge are hoping that the presence of such an esteemed name as Toyota in such close proximity to Highway 401 will act as a catalyst

Although Kitchener's economy is not primarily agrarian, pastoral scenes like this one can be found throughout the area. Photo by Dave Prichard/ First Light

for industrial growth in the area, just as Goodrich, Kaufman, and Electrohome earlier had such an important impact upon different sections of Kitchener.

Toyota's decision to build near Kitchener is perhaps the most significant development in Kitchener's industrial expansion during the last decade. Although the plant lies just outside its municipal boundaries, there is little doubt that Toyota chose the location because of the area's broad industrial base. Japanese officials understood that even such an immense plant would not upset an economic balance predicated on diversity. Kitchener was not susceptible to the economic changes that plagued other communities. Currently over 30 companies with links to the auto industry in the Kitchener-Waterloo-Cambridge area employ over 11,000 workers. Should Toyota reach "Auto Pact" status—meaning that 60 percent of the parts used in their vehicles must be Canadian made—Kitchener would reap tremendous benefits. When at full production, Toyota expects to produce 50,000 cars per year at the new facility.

Observers are hoping that free trade will bring with it benefits similar to those engendered by the 1965 Auto Pact. Soon after the treaty was signed, Budd Automotive Company of Canada announced plans to build a $22 million plant on Homer Watson Boulevard. Company officials cited "metal working skills, excellent work attitudes, good vocational training and engineering at the University of Waterloo as major location factors in favour of Kitchener." Kitchenerites were delighted, knowing full well that the automotive treaty almost guaranteed the profitability of auto-related businesses in Canada. Their faith in the agreement was not misplaced. By October 1971 Budd Canada employed 2,120 in three shifts. General Springs, a company which specialized in the manufacture of seating mechanisms for automobiles, also took advantage of the growth opportunity and moved from its downtown location to a site near the Budd plant. Now known as Lear-Siegler, the firm has become an integral part of Kitchener's auto parts industry.

Despite the number of large auto-related businesses in Kitchener, the city is not overly dependent upon them. In fact, less than 10 percent of the local work force is engaged in such businesses. And civic officials like it that way. While they would not discourage a specific business from locating here, they remain ever mindful that economic diversity is crucial in evening out the peaks and valleys of unemployment, in providing a consistent tax base, and in attracting other companies—customers or suppliers—to the city.

If one theme can be identified to characterize Kitchener's industrial development, it would have to be diversity. In one word, diversity explains the phenomenon of "Busy Berlin," just as it explains how Kitchener became such a major economic power locally, provincially, nationally, and, increasingly, internationally. With an economic base spread broadly from heavy industry to social services and including hundreds of businesses engaged in the manufacture, sale, and distribution of just about any product imaginable, Kitchener's present is very much the product of its past. And, as in the days of "Busy Berlin," it is a high-quality product, indeed.

George M. DeBus was a well-known hairdresser who set up shop in Berlin during the 1860s. Although he provided a broad range of services, he was especially popular among the bearded men of the community for his skill at dyeing whiskers "a permanent colour." According to local historian W.V. Uttley, he also provided another special service. He was the village dentist, "and extracted teeth without the use of an anaesthetic, unless it was a nip of old rye."

Thankfully those days are gone, and the people of Kitchener enjoy an array of health services unsurpassed in most regions of the country. Two large, fully equipped general hospitals, an innovative health-care village specializing in chronic care, a number of specialty clinics, homes for the elderly and the handicapped, and a host of physicians, surgeons, and dentists provide the people of Kitchener with a caring atmosphere and the services they need to maintain a healthy lifestyle. But it wasn't always that way.

People used to rely on either prayer or folk

INVESTING IN TOMORROW

The contemporary design of the YWCA sign contrasts greatly with the older architectural style of the Frederick Street building occupied by the organization. Photo by Judy-Ann Cazemier/First Light

remedies to keep them in good health. When an epidemic struck, there was little anyone could do but to bury the dead, burn the possessions of the dying, quarantine the households of the stricken, and hope for the best. Standard medical practices of the day, including bloodletting, opium, mercury, sweat baths, and various tonics, were ineffective. When these attempts failed, old Mennonite folk cures became a last resort. For example, it was common knowledge that boiling a fox lung in water and drinking the potion would cure asthma. By eating the leaf of a male dandelion on nine successive mornings, those afflicted with consumption (tuberculosis) would regain their health. Those unfortunate enough to contract TB during the winter months made up for the shortage of dandelions by drinking an unsavoury tea made from the feces of a black horse. Children with whooping cough were expected to recover if they ate a piece of bread made by a woman whose married name was the same as her maiden name.

Despite these remedies, one out of every 12 deaths was from tuberculosis. Diphtheria commonly killed 50 percent of those it infected, while typhoid killed 20 percent and measles and scarlet fever 10 percent each. So loose were med-

ical standards that the sole factor determining the level of a surgeon's skill was the speed with which he completed his operations. The best surgeons could amputate a limb—the only solution to a number of medical problems—in about one minute. Since most operations were performed without ether or chloroform, and the wounds were seared with heat to stem the flow of blood, speed was essential to prevent death by shock.

The first doctors in Berlin were among the community's most prominent citizens. In fact, when Waterloo County was created in 1852, the people elected Dr. John Scott as the first reeve, a position equivalent to the mayor of a larger municipality. Dr. William Pipe—"six foot three in his stockings," according to Uttley—was the first mayor of the Town of Berlin. Henry Lackner, who set up a medical practice in 1876, served in the Ontario Legislature, and every generation of the Lackner family since has seen at least one member become a doctor.

The first Board of Health was appointed shortly after Berlin was elevated to village status in 1854. Comprised of nine citizens, its mandate was "to provide for the health of the village against the spread of contagious disease, and to regulate the interment of the dead." The wording reflected the memories of a cholera epidemic which had wiped out a substantial portion of the population of neighbouring Galt only 20 years before.

In its early days the Board of Health dealt with a wide variety of complaints from the citizens and was not opposed to issuing a few of its own. Indeed, Berliners complained about everything from cesspools and privies to manure piles, water supplies, inadequate drainage at the market, spitting on the boardwalks "especially outside of hotels," and the "bad smells" emanating from Schneider's Creek. In 1891, "much to the relief and pleasure of the Board," Berlin Council finally heeded the warnings of health officials and voted to install sewers. Other complaints led the Board to advocate creation of a water commission, which was frequently criticized for allowing "too many snakes and worms in the water supply."

The community took its first real leap forward in 1894, when plans were announced for the Berlin and Waterloo General Hospital. The initiative to build a community hospital actually began one year before, when a group of concerned citizens began soliciting donations. A ripple of excitement went through the community when Waterloo distiller Joseph E. Seagram donated 14 acres of land near the Berlin-Waterloo boarder as a hospital site. He had originally purchased the site, called Greenbush, as a place to construct an estate. But when he discovered that the site lay entirely in Berlin and not in his beloved Waterloo, he decided to dispose of the land. His only stipulations were that the site be forever occupied by a hospital and that no person ever be denied access on religious, financial, or ethnic grounds.

On September 19, 1894, the cornerstone of the new hospital was laid by Ontario Provincial Secretary J.M. Gibson. Soon an impressive structure with room for 50 patients emerged.

The people of Berlin and Waterloo had contributed $10,000 and $5,000 re-

FACING PAGE:
Ambulances transport some of the more than 180 patients who end up in Kitchener-Waterloo Hospital's emergency room every day. Photo by Judy-Ann Cazemier/First Light

The $37.5-million Freeport Health Care Village, shown under construction here, was officially opened in 1989. Photo by Winston Fraser

spectively to the construction fund. Hospital ownership and government were in the form of a trust, headed by George Randall of Waterloo and John Fennell of Berlin, which included most of the leading citizens in the two communities. Payment of a $5 membership fee bought local citizens one vote. A life membership cost $100, a substantial sum in those days. From its inception, the gifts of private citizens and local organizations were an integral part of the hospital's development. In its first annual report the trust reported gifts of food, linen, kitchen utensils, magazines, and a wheelbarrow.

By 1898 the hospital had become a local fixture, but it had one peculiar problem—a lack of patients. Many had argued that the building was too ambitious a project from the outset, and when a government inspector reported that it held only nine patients at one point, they were not surprised. Wealthy citizens still preferred to convalesce in their homes, and the first patients were those who generally could not afford the costs associated with being ill. But by 1913 the combined populations of Berlin and Waterloo had almost doubled, and an additional 70 beds were needed to keep up with the demand. In 1920 the Kaufman family of Berlin donated a new residence for nurses. The Breithaupt, Lang, Bowlby, and Rumpel families—all prominent business owners—also made significant contributions, setting a precedent of public support that has been maintained to this day. In 1924, however, as equipment requirements and a proposed expansion placed a considerable financial burden on the hospital trust, the cities of Kitchener and Waterloo assumed joint ownership and appointed a Hospital Commission.

In 1935 a three-storey addition housing the departments of obstetrics and pediatrics was built west of the main hospital. Called "the Pavilion," the building added 52 beds and 21 basinettes to the hospital's capacity. A new x-ray department also was included. The addition was timely, for between 1940 and 1945 the number of patients requiring treatment nearly doubled. Under the guidance of Commission Chairman C.N. Weber, a nine-storey addition was begun in 1948. The cornerstone was laid by Minister of Health Paul Martin and the completed structure dedicated in 1951 by Canada's governor-general, Viscount Alexander of Tunis. The original hospital building was refurbished, provided with 110 chronic care beds, and christened the Kathleen Scott Pavilion in honour of a long-time hospital superintendent.

Over the past 30 years Kitchener-Waterloo Hospital has been shaped by many influences. Fluctuations in government funding and control, inroads in medical treatment, the social influences of the community, and innovations in health care have had a tremendous impact upon the institution.

Although the hospital continued to grow, with multi-million dollar additions in 1962 and 1967, by 1976 it had become clear that some services would have to be shared with the Roman Catholic St. Mary's General Hospital. Today a rationalization program will see the two institutions maintain a constructive partnership into the next century, despite the differences in their original mandates and development.

Former K-W Hospital President Joseph de Mora notes that it costs over $300 per day to support a patient in hospital. Medical technology has become so specialized that 80 percent of the hospital's annual budget goes toward staff salaries. The hospital's approximately 600 beds accommodate over 20,000 patients a year. The emergency room treats over 180 patients daily, and 17 outpatient clinics, well known for their facilities, receive many referrals from outside the region.

Like private business in the community, K-W Hospital is advocating several new initiatives. Gone are the days when hospitals could rely solely on government support, says director of planning Pat Cawley. Operating funds may be generated through joint ventures with local companies or other business opportunities in the future. Several years ago, de Mora suggested that local hospitals could develop and run employee assistance programs for private industry. It is felt that programs on stress reduction, drug abuse, and psychological counselling may be more acceptable to employees if provided by an objective source. Such "outreach clinics," supported by private business, could provide operating funds for the hospital in the future.

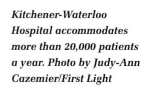

Kitchener-Waterloo Hospital accommodates more than 20,000 patients a year. Photo by Judy-Ann Cazemier/First Light

In sharp contrast to its non-denominational counterpart, St. Mary's Hospital was opened by the Roman Catholic Sisters of St. Joseph in 1924. The order purchased the property from the Sisters of Providence of St. Vincent de Paul in 1921. At the time, the site was on the extreme southern fringe of the city—a grassy knoll surrounded by nothing but farmland. With 50 patients, the three-storey, 152-bed facility was immediately praised as a tremendous asset for the city. W.V. Uttley called the new hospital "one of the Dominion's best." By the end of its first year, a total of 920 patients had been admitted.

As a denominational institution, St. Mary's was unable to secure the funds necessary for any full-scale expansion and remained content to simply upgrade the existing facilities from time to time. In fact, the hospital operated at capacity for many years until a major expansion became an absolute necessity in 1962. By the time the new structure was completed, the nine-storey addition had grown to occupy 10 city housing lots and provided space for 238 beds. The original building was converted to offices and a resource centre. Today St. Mary's has a capacity of 354 beds and admits over 14,000 patients annually.

Despite the large numbers of patients, neither hospital has undergone a major expansion for almost two decades, although both are in the process of planning additions and both are enthusiastic about a plan to rationalize services over the

With their school as a backdrop, a pair of Kitchener high school students make a pleasing portrait of youth. Photo by Dave Prichard/First Light

In addition to its applied arts, business, health services, and technology courses, Conestoga College offers a number of apprenticeship programs. Photo by Dave Prichard/First Light

next decade. According to St. Mary's Executive Director Bruce Antonello, rationalization means the two hospitals are no longer "going to be everything to everybody." Under the terms of the agreement, K-W Hospital will specialize in obstetrics, reproductive medicine, and neonatal care. St. Mary's will specialize in pediatrics and has plans to establish a rheumatoid disease centre. In both cases the hospitals are looking to enhance their reputations as progressive health-care institutions. As Antonello says, "Even to stand still we have to grow."

Although K-W and St. Mary's hospitals have been providing the people of Kitchener with the basic health services they have required for generations, they have not been the only hospitals in the area. In fact, much of the community's attention during the last half of the 1980s was focused upon the transformation of the old Freeport Sanatorium into an innovative health-care village—a unique hospital on the leading edge of chronic care in Canada.

In his 1987 history of Freeport Hospital, *Caring on the Grand,* Peter Conrad noted, "throughout its history, Freeport has generated a special dedication among local citizens." That dedication began in 1908 when the Reverend F. E. Oberlander and Dr. J. F. Honsberger formed an "Anti-Consumption League" to encourage interest in the need for an institution in which those with tuberculosis could be treated. As a result of their efforts, the Berlin Sanatorium Association was formed in 1911. This group convinced Berlin Council to purchase the Shantz property on the bank of the Grand River at Freeport. The estate included 15 acres of land, a solid stone house, and an ample supply of water.

In May 1915 the City of Berlin assumed control of the institution and prepared to receive the first patients. But the Military Hospitals Commission intervened. Needing space to treat soldiers who contracted TB during World War I, the commission occupied Freeport from 1916 until 1920 when it was turned over to the City of Kitchener. At that time the Waterloo County Health Association assumed responsibility for the institution, and the 61-bed facility was finally opened to the public. Over the next 20 years, Freeport added 76 beds to complete the transition from renovated farm house to modern hospital.

By the end of World War II, Freeport served five counties and had become famous for its extensive preventive programs such as diagnostic chest clinics and tuberculin skin testing in schools. But medical advances and antibiotics soon began reducing the need for specialized sanatoria, and by 1957 Freeport had begun admitting chronic and rehabilitative patients. This was indeed fortunate, because the need for chronic-care beds grew rapidly throughout the 1960s, and by 1970 the tuberculosis division of the hospital was being phased out. Reflecting this change, the old sanatorium was renamed Freeport Hospital.

In the years since, Freeport has established itself as Waterloo Region's chronic/rehabilitative hospital, specializing in the treatment of such varied illnesses as multiple sclerosis and Alzheimer's disease. The $37.5-million Freeport Health Care Village, a continuation of the hospital's tradition of revolutionary health care, was officially opened by Ontario Premier David Peterson in 1989. At the opening ceremony the premier lauded the people of the community for their generous donations to the building fund. A recent article about the new facility summed up its mandate, noting how the village concept replaced a regular hospital setting "with a home-like atmosphere, where the patients' individual lifestyles are the prime consideration." As another writer put it, "How many hospitals can boast having an ice cream parlor, a swimming pool, outside courtyards, an indoor-outdoor theatre and a bar?"

Together, the Freeport Health Care Village, K-W Hospital, and St. Mary's Hospital have a long and colourful history. But their significance is hardly limited to the past. With a growing and aging population, Kitchener will need the services these institutions provide for decades to come.

Although they are the dominant health-care institutions in the community, there is more to health care than the three hospitals. Many dentists maintain offices in Kitchener, practising everything from orthodontia to denture therapy. Dental surgeons operate both in their offices and at the hospitals. Numerous chiropractors have established practices and nursing homes provide care for the elderly. The Waterloo Regional Health Unit provides a number of services, including infectious disease control, school health and dental care, nutrition services, and a first-rate home care program. The Rotary Children's Centre and the Sunbeam Residential Development Centre provide services for physically and mentally handicapped children. A recent phenomenon, "after hours" clinics operated out of local doctors' offices, have helped ease the burden on crowded emergency rooms and made medical treatment as accessible as the local convenience store.

Nobody enjoys being sick. But the people of Kitchener have always been comforted by the fact that should they become ill, a sophisticated and highly respected network of services is in place to help care for them. After all, Kitchener has established a respected reputation as a community that cares.

Like health care, education has been a key ingredient in many of the successes Kitchener has experienced through the years. From the industrial prowess of "Busy Berlin" to the political success of William Lyon Mackenzie King, the technological wonders of the modern automobile industry, and the establishment of three universities and a community college, the people of Kitchener have become as famous for their know-how as for their energy and initiative. As in the field of health care, however and just like in many other centres of academic excellence, Kitchener's long tradition in the field of education had humble beginnings.

Bishop Benjamin Eby opened the community's first school in the winter of 1818. Teaching in German, he used the Bible as his text book. Later, when the task of teaching grew more onerous, he was assisted by anyone who volunteered, including "roaming men . . . old soldiers . . . masons and carpenters." Despite this, Eby's school ran much more smoothly than others. Another school, begun some years later by James Derry, closed in 1837 due to heating problems and the "imbibing habits" of the teacher. The first secondary school, grandly called The Wellington Institute, was opened by John Fayette in 1840. He is believed to have been the first person to teach grammar and to display a map in his classroom. But the idea of advanced learning never caught on, Fayette fell into debt, and he skipped town one step ahead of his creditors.

In those days most learning was done in the home. But even when people did learn to read, it was often a challenge to obtain reading material. This problem was solved when a Mechanic's Institute was opened at the rear of Henry Eby's print shop in 1854. Within a decade the library had a collection of over 1,000

Students enjoy some fresh air on the St. Timothy School campus on Pioneer Drive. Photo by Winston Fraser

English and German titles. The membership fee was one dollar and books were exchanged each Saturday night. Unfortunately, the entire collection was destroyed by fire in the late 1860s, and for many years there was no local book repository. The Berlin Public Library was not established until 1884, and only after long periods of planning and two Carnegie grants was a large and modern library built at the corner of Queen and Weber streets. In 1909 the Library Board entered uncharted territory when it hired Mabel Dunham, the first professional librarian to run a library in Ontario. Since that time the library has acquired a fully computerized collection of over 400,000 books.

Today the Kitchener Public Library provides numerous community services. Meeting rooms and a large auditorium are used for everything from political debates to club meetings, concerts, card parties, lectures, readings by visiting authors, and receptions. A large collection of audio-visual materials are available, including video tapes, films, records, tapes, compact discs, and slides. The Grace Schmidt Room of Local History contains many rare documents and books chronicling the history of Kitchener. In addition, the archives contain the com-

The Kitchener campus of Conestoga College of Applied Arts and Technology was established in 1967 at Doon, now a part of Kitchener. The college boasts five other campuses. Photo by Dave Prichard/First Light

plete photo collections of the Waterloo Historical Society and the Chamber of Commerce. Information services are also available to provide facts and figures about any topic imaginable. Reference facilities serve everyone from students to lawyers and businesspeople.

The establishment of the Mechanic's Institute was crucial to the education of Berliners in the days before formal learning was deemed a top priority. In fact, at the time of Fayette's adventure, Berlin was known as School Section 5 of Waterloo Township. It did not have the population or resources to administer its own school system. This changed dramatically when Central School was built in 1857. The community's first "real" school, it opened the doors to a bright future for many youngsters. In 1910 the school, still in operation on Frederick Street, was renamed in honour of the late principal Jeremiah Suddaby. But by then there were a number of other schools: King Edward (1886), Courtland Avenue (1890), and Margaret Avenue (1895). Victoria School was opened in 1912. The first "separate" (Roman Catholic) school was opened by the Reverend George Laufhuber in 1859, but a permanent building was not built until 1874. Although it was not given a specific name, it quickly became known as St. Mary's due to its location next to the prominent Catholic parish. Before 1930 three more separate schools had been built: Sacred Heart (1912), St. Joseph's (1921), and St. John's (1929). Today there are 23 separate schools and 35 public schools in Kitchener. In addition, there are two separate high schools and five public high schools. All are part of two larger regional school boards (public and separate) created by the Ontario government in the late 1960s.

The first public high school in the community was the Berlin High School, built in 1876. Household science and technical studies were added to the curriculum shortly after the turn of the century. Before World War I, students from Waterloo were required to purchase their education from the Berlin School Board but in 1914, a provincial order in council enlarged the High School District to include Waterloo, allowing children from Waterloo free access to the facilities. The name was changed to Kitchener and Waterloo Collegiate and Vocational School in 1923, and today is commonly called "KCI." Although most graduates immediately entered the local work force, it was quite common for others to attend the well-known Euler Business College.

Established in 1900, the business school was affiliated with the Federated Business Colleges of Ontario. William D. Euler, the principal, purchased the school when the federation was dissolved and renamed it the Berlin Business College. According to W.V. Uttley, "the best business methods were taught and the keynote was thoroughness." A large number of Berlin/Kitchener's leading businessmen —including many still operating successful local companies—learned their skills at Euler's school. But Euler himself was unable to continue teaching after 1917 because of his election to Parliament in the famous "conscription" election. Later, when his friend, erstwhile Berliner William Lyon Mackenzie King, became Prime Minister, Euler was appointed Minister of Trade and Commerce. Although he won re-election in 1940, he ran afoul of the Prime Minister, who no longer wanted him in the Commons, and he was appointed to the Senate. L.O. Breithaupt, who would later be appointed Lieutenant Governor of Ontario, succeeded him in the resulting by-election.

Widely respected as the oldest educational institution in Kitchener, St. Jerome's High School lost that position to its long-time rival KCI in the spring of

Wilfrid Laurier University's Frank C. Peters Building is one of the more modern campus structures. Photo by Judy-Ann Cazemier

1990. The flagship of Catholic education was closed, to be replaced by the sparkling multi-million dollar Resurrection Catholic Secondary School in Waterloo. The story of St. Jerome's is very familiar to the people of Kitchener. The original school was opened as a "college" in a small log cabin in St. Agatha—a small crossroads community outside Kitchener—in 1865 by the Reverend Louis Funcken, a member of the Congregation of the Resurrection. Before long the college was overcrowded, and Father Funcken purchased a brick house near St. Mary's church in Berlin and added a classroom wing. To finance the purchase, he completed a lecture tour of the northern U.S. Upon his return he found the college in disarray. Most of the staff had left for health reasons and for several years Father Funcken was the only priest at St. Jerome's. But through his energetic efforts, the situation improved. In the ensuing years many additions to the college were made. When the founder died in 1890, he left behind a legacy that would never be erased.

In the late 1980s the decision to close St. Jerome's generated a great deal of controversy. Some felt the original name should remain out of respect for the school's long tradition of academic and athletic excellence. As a form of compromise, the school board decided to name the new school after Father Funcken's religious order and to change the school's symbol from a roaring lion to a phoenix—symbolic of the new institution which had risen from the remnants of the old one.

The local "Y" is, as always, a reliable source of education, guidance and recreation. Photo by Dave Prichard/First Light

Of course, the St. Jerome's name still exists on the campus of the University of Waterloo. When the original St. Jerome's College completed the transition from college to high school, the school sought an affiliation with the University of Ottawa for the purpose of granting degrees. A site called Kingsdale was purchased on the eastern outskirts of Kitchener, and a large, new college building was constructed. It was officially opened by Ontario Premier Leslie Frost in 1953. Meanwhile, the Lutheran Seminary in Waterloo, which since 1925 had been affiliated with the University of Western Ontario as Waterloo College, was looking to expand.

The race between the two schools for university affiliation caused the creation of the University of Waterloo in 1957, and in 1960 the two rivals became affiliates of the new institution. But the Lutheran Synod, exercising its

The Kitchener Collegiate
Institute prepares its
graduates for entry into
the modern work force.
Photo by Dave Prichard/
First Light

prerogative, overruled its Board of Governors, and Waterloo College withdrew from the agreement. Forced to choose, Waterloo College President J.G. Hagey chose the University of Waterloo, and over time transformed what he had once dismissed as a "matchbook on a farm" into an internationally respected school.

St. Jerome's, meanwhile, obtained accreditation as a university in its own right and served as a model for other religious denominations. In a very short time the university grew to include Renison (Anglican), St. Paul's (United), and Conrad Grebel (Mennonite) colleges. Conrad Grebel is the only Mennonite college in the world with a complete university affiliation. Of course, it was not long before Waterloo College became Waterloo Lutheran University, and later Wilfrid Laurier University.

Although all of these institutions are located in Kitchener's twin city, Waterloo, it may be argued that the long history of St. Jerome's College—and its desire to keep higher learning a priority in the community—was ultimately responsible for the establishment of not one, but three highly respected universities in the area. Today the University of Waterloo is, in terms of student enrolment, the seventh-largest university in Canada, and its affiliates, including St. Jerome's, enjoy wide respect in academic circles.

Wilfrid Laurier University, although much smaller, offers a broad range of disciplines, including arts, science, music, and social work. Its School of Business and Economics is the most well-known, however. The Waterloo Lutheran Seminary is still affiliated with the school, preparing theology students for the Master of Divinity degree. A Small Business Consulting Service puts the skills of students to work on real problems in the business world, and the university continues to enjoy a good relationship with the University of Waterloo.

The three universities, however, are not the only institutions of higher learning in the area. The Conestoga College of Applied Arts and Technology was established at Doon (now part of Kitchener) in 1967. The centrepiece of the 137-acre campus is the Conestoga Centre, a sports and recreation complex which includes an Olympic-size ice surface. With five other campuses (Cambridge, Guelph, Clinton, Stratford, and Waterloo) Conestoga College continues to have a major impact upon education in the area.

The college is an acknowledged leader in the fields of applied arts, business, health services, and especially technology. The school specializes in telecommunications education and has broken new ground in the area of computer assisted design/computer assisted manufacturing (CAD/CAM) robotics training. In addition, a number of apprenticeship programs are offered. Each year an increasing number of mature students participate in continuing education programs, either upgrading their present skills or simply pursuing general interests. Conestoga's Employer Centred Training program provides specific courses for use by local businesses and industries. A program called Futures accommodates

Wilfrid Laurier University (previously named Waterloo College and Waterloo Lutheran University) offers courses in the arts, sciences, music, social work, business, and economics. Photo by Dave Prichard/ First Light

unemployed young people between the ages of 16 and 24. Ontario skills development officials, based at the college's office in Kitchener, provide training guidance and financial assistance to students.

Says College President Kenneth Hunter, "I believe education will move away from grades and time-based courses to a method of education called 'Mastery Learning.' Instead of trying to reach 60 percent to pass, students will stay with a particular subject until they have mastered it, and then move on to the next subject. We are already testing this method, and results are reaching close to 100 percent." Obviously, with 53 full-time diploma and certificate programs, 11 apprenticeship programs, 5,000 full-time students, and 29,000 registrants in continuing education courses, Conestoga College will continue to have a major impact, not just upon Kitchener but upon much of southern Ontario.

Education in Kitchener and the surrounding area has earned renown for its ability and willingness to change with the times. It is not surprising, therefore, that it is continuing to do so faster than in most other jurisdictions. Co-operative education as promoted by the University of Waterloo has been such a success that the local school boards have begun to introduce similar programs at the secondary school level. As Henry Bloos, a co-operative education officer at the Waterloo County Board of Education, puts it, "The Agricultural Revolution lasted 6,000 years, the Industrial Revolution 300 years, and now we are in the Information Age, a time which is bringing change like never before, and educators cannot do it alone. All parts of the community have to work together if we are to meet the demands of the future." Peter Hicknell, superintendent of education at the Waterloo Region Roman Catholic School Board agrees, noting, "Curricula are being revised to reflect the real world. At one time, learning was by memory, but that is changing. Students, who may expect to have between two and four careers, need to learn to think for themselves."

Kitchener's schools possess the resources to help students think for themselves, and necessities like computer instruction are a vital part of the learning experience. Instead of being confined to rows of desks in a classroom, students spend part of their time on the job, identifying their skills and discovering the types of work they enjoy. Statistics show that of every 100 students entering ninth grade, 18 will attend a university, 19 will enter a community college, and the remaining 63 will move immediately into the work force upon graduating. The figures obviously speak for themselves. Business and industry are faced with the fact that education, if it is to succeed in a fast-paced world, must assume some of the responsibility of educating the work force. After all, without education the quality of our products and services will deteriorate and make us uncompetitive in an increasingly competitive world.

Health care and education—two services often taken for granted—have taken on increasing significance as the city approaches a new century. And the people of Kitchener have responded to the challenge, as they have for generations, putting a long and valuable history—and the wealth of knowledge contained within it—to constructive use in solving the problems of tomorrow.

Tuesday, May 2, 1871, was not an ordinary spring day in Berlin. People had spent the day before decorating their homes and businesses with evergreen boughs and German and British flags. The large Hamilton Band had arrived in full uniform that evening, causing quite a commotion as they marched through the village. No, it wasn't just an ordinary spring day. Young Louis Breithaupt, a member of one of Berlin's leading families, wrote in his diary:

Today was a public holiday as there was a great peace jubilee in town. This peace jubilee refers to the peace which has been concluded between Germany and France [marking the end of the Franco-Prussian War]. All the stores and businesses of both towns [Berlin and Waterloo] were closed . . . There were from 10,000 to 12,000 visitors in Berlin today.

The great Friedensfest (Peace Festival) of 1871 marked the beginning of a cultural tradition in Berlin/Kitchener, which would come full circle in

5 PAINTING FROM A PALETTE OF CULTURES

Visitors to Doon Pioneer Village will see part of Kitchener's past re-created. Photo by Glen Jones

the late 1960s with an annual Oktoberfest celebrating the community's German culture and traditions. *Sängerfeste,* or German singing festivals, were another tremendously popular attraction. Tens of thousands of visitors came to Berlin to hear German folk songs, choral presentations, and instrumental interpretations of works by the great German composers. And, as supporters of Oktoberfest would point out 100 years later, such festivals couldn't help but bolster the local economy. The fact that *Sängerfeste* usually lasted three days encouraged people from far and wide to attend the event, spending money liberally.

Although bands, choirs, and musical societies didn't really begin to blossom as important cultural institutions in Berlin until after the first *Sängerfest,* they existed and played an important role in the community from its earliest days. The first mention of a musical group in the area appeared in the *Duetsche Canadier* in 1845, when the newspaper noted the Bridgeport and Berlin Band "had given the citizens of Berlin proof of their musical skill."

The Berlin Band's first instruments were purchased by private subscription, a common method of supporting community activities in those days. But the band was not able to meet the financial obligations of travelling to play at events in other communities. The instruments remained in storage for several years until tavern owner Henry Glebe organized the Berliner Musikband and purchased them. Local music historians agree that Glebe likely formed the band to entertain the patrons of his hotel.

With so many similar establishments in the downtown core, Glebe felt that he had to provide an alternative to card playing and other popular pastimes. This is confirmed by the Kitchener Musical Society's historical outline of local band activities. The authors pointed out that Glebe's band "played mainly for pleasure, although there were sometimes additional incentives . . . They were always ready to serenade the many places where free beer might be expected." One can only assume that the beer flowed freely at Glebe's hotel and that this kept the band away from rival hoteliers.

Another hotelier, William Kaiser, a noted bandsman who had emigrated to Berlin from Detroit, organized the United Band. Like Glebe, he was less concerned about the cultural development of the community than he was with the entertainment of his patrons. He recognized the need to attract attention to his establishment, and he understood that providing good music would help him do it.

In 1875 a spectacular bandfest was held in Berlin. Although the band members were quite adept with strings and percussion instruments, the Berlin Bandfest revealed—for the first time—the pleasing sound and versatility of reed instruments. The local bandmasters saw great potential in the instruments and decided that their bands must be expanded to accommodate the new sound. The immediate result was a doubling of the size of the local bands, from a maximum of 15 members to almost 30. Soon the resonant tones of the saxophone, clarinet, and bassoon had expanded the abilities of each band immensely. People began coming to Berlin just to hear them play.

The introduction of the new instruments added a spark to the local musical scene. In 1875 Kaiser's band was absorbed into the newly formed Berlin Musical Society Band, which quickly gained notoriety for its ability to adapt to any type of music. Many of the members came from Glebe's band. Their versatility—undoubtedly a product of their increased proficiency with reed instruments—signalled a new era in the musical life of the community.

Under the direction of John S. Smith, a local grocer and an accomplished clarinettist, the new Berlin Musical Society Band developed further, until in 1877 it was named the band of the 29th Infantry Regiment of the Canadian Militia, a significant honor at the time. A rash of post-Civil War Fenian raids and heightened Canada-U.S. tensions arising from trade and boundary disputes put the militia in a position of prominence. A band like the one from Berlin helped to boost the morale of the soldiers and added to the characteristic military pageantry. It also didn't hurt that the group played a brand of music which inspired the general population. In fact, the impact of the band became evident in 1879, when the group won $400 in a musical competition held to celebrate Guelph's cityhood. The band reached the pinnacle of its popularity in 1899, when it played a critically acclaimed concert at Toronto's Massey Hall. It was greeted upon its return to Berlin with the pomp and ceremony generally accorded only the most important of visitors.

At one point, the Berlin Musical Society Band's conductor was Noah Zeller, an uncle of Berlin native and department store founder Walter P. Zeller. According to local historian W.V. Uttley, "Mr. Zeller's musicians played a Beethoven symphony or a Wagnerian overture with as much skill as any popular air." And

The Kitchener-Waterloo Symphony Orchestra, with its tours and special engagements, is an outstanding contributor to the cultural life of the city and the province. Photo by Dave Prichard/First Light

they excelled at popular music as well. Shortly after the turn of the century, *Saturday Night* magazine commented, "Of all the bands which visit Toronto, except professional bands, it is the best." Sadly, the musical society lost all of its instruments, and an invaluable music library containing arrangements dating back to the mid-nineteenth century, when the King Street band hall was destroyed by fire in 1959. Much of Kitchener's musical heritage was lost forever in the flames.

This substantial background in music, enabled Kitchener to gain recognition as home to three present-day, award-winning, drum-and-bugle corps. The oldest operates under the name Northstar Youth Organization. Founded in 1969 as the Dutch Boy Cadets, the organization today is divided into three groups: Dutch Boy Pre-Cadets for children aged 6 to 10, the Cadets of Dutch Boy for those 10 to 14, and the Dutch Boy Junior Drum and Bugle Corps for those 14 to

21. A second group, the Kiwanis Kavaliers, grew out of a Dutch Boy Cadets' membership drive in 1971. When more applications were received than expected, a feeder corps was begun. In 1972 the Twin City Kiwanis Club sponsored the group. A third group is the all-female Ventures Corps, commonly called "the ladies in gold." If you listen closely on summer Saturday mornings, you may hear the sounds of these youngsters practising their drills on local sports fields.

Violinists with the Kitchener-Waterloo Symphony rehearse before a concert engagement. Photo by Dave Prichard/First Light

The founding of the Berlin Philharmonic and Orchestra Society in the early 1880s was a direct result of Berlin's tradition of successful music festivals. Under the direction of Professor Theodor Zoellner, the new society was nothing if not ambitious. Performances of Mendelssohn's *Lobesgesang* and Handel's *Messiah* met with rave reviews. Zoellner himself was chosen as conductor of the International Sängerfest in 1886. Later, when it became obvious that the group was setting a standard of choral excellence in the area, it became known as the K-W Philharmonic Choir. The name change was symbolic of the group's intention to focus on singing as opposed to instrumental performances.

When Professor Zoellner died in the early 1920s, he was replaced by L.J. Yule, the recently hired supervisor of music in the local public schools. Under his direction, the choir won first prize at the prestigious Canadian Music Festival in Toronto. In later years the choir began a program of regular collaboration with the K-W Symphony Orchestra, and together the two institutions have maintained a strong presence in the community to the present. Every year some of the most popular programs at the beautiful Centre in the Square theatre arts complex are put on by the combined choir and symphony.

Today the tradition of fine choral music is upheld by many groups, including the Kitchener Bach Choir, the Concordia Club Choirs, the Menno Singers, the Inter-Mennonite Children's Choir, the Twin City Harmonizers, the Schneider Male Chorus, the K-W Opera Guild, and the Gilbert and Sullivan Society.

Although the K-W Symphony Orchestra has without question become one of the most important cultural institutions in the community, it has a relatively short history. This is undoubtedly the result of the community's penchant for choral and band music. In the past, orchestras were commonly formed only for special events and were usually disbanded shortly thereafter. On other, less auspicious occasions, the local bands provided more than adequate entertainment. In fact, the community was so satisfied with its bands that a formal attempt to establish an orchestra of full symphonic proportions was not made until 1926. Although the orchestra was promising, the conductor, James J. Galloway, left for Hamilton after only three years and the organization, unable to withstand the loss, was discontinued.

Although the unsuccessful orchestra had won numerous converts to classical music and engendered a level of support which surprised many, the idea of a symphony lay dormant until 1944, when Kitchener insurance agency owner W.A. "Archie" Bernhardt rekindled the flame. Bernhardt felt that Kitchener could never be culturally complete until it had an orchestra. He was under no illusions about the simplicity of his task, however, recalling, "Anyone even suggesting a symphony orchestra had always been reminded of the great difficulties entailed in such an undertaking. Usually that's as far as the matter would go." But Bernhardt refused to let the matter drop, and convened a meeting of the local musical community, where a decision was made to proceed. Dr. Glenn Kruspe, director of the K-W Philharmonic Choir and a man widely respected for his musical taste and acute knowledge of musical theory, was chosen as the first conductor.

According to Bernhardt, Dr. Kruspe was "the most suitable man we could find over quite an area." He was also very popular among local musicians, many of whom volunteered immediately to join the orchestra. This time the symphony was a success, and it became an integral part of the local culture. Kruspe, the man most responsible for the symphony's success in its infancy, conducted the orchestra until 1960 when he was succeeded by a distinguished French musician, Frederick Pohl.

Raffi Armenian, who remains the symphony's conductor and music director, was handed the baton in 1971. After receiving his musical training in Vienna, he accepted a position as assistant conductor of the Atlantic Symphony in Halifax, Nova Scotia, before coming to Kitchener. Under his direction the K-W Sym-

The Kitchener Memorial Auditorium hosts a variety of events. Photo by Winston Fraser

phony Orchestra has exceeded the wildest expectations of its founders, becoming one of Canada's most respected orchestras.

With a repertoire that embraces classical symphonies, chamber music, and the works of great modern composers, it pleases audiences of all ages and musical preferences. The "Masterpiece Series" caters to those who favour classical composers like Mozart, Wagner, Beethoven, Tchaikovsky, and Brahms. The "Pops Series" combines the music of the symphony with visual spectacles, including performances by the National Ballet of Canada and screenings of classic movies. In one instance, the symphony performed Charlie Chaplin's own score to one of his films. The "Sunday Serenade Series" brings the light classics to relaxed audiences on Sunday afternoons, while a series entitled "Baroque and Beyond" brings to life the music of the Baroque era. In 1991 this series commemorates the bicentenary of Mozart by focussing on composers from countries through which Mozart travelled.

In collaboration with the Philharmonic Choir, the orchestra has also produced stirring renditions of the traditional masterworks by Mendelssohn and Handel as well as Haydn's *Creation,* Verdi's *Requiem*, and J.S. Bach's *St. John's Passion.* The symphony also stages musical programs for children designed to get them interested in music. The presence of the symphony in the community encouraged the formation of the Kitchener-Waterloo Symphony Youth Orchestra and the highly acclaimed Canadian Chamber Ensemble, which has toured worldwide. In short, the K-W Symphony Orchestra has become one of the greatest goodwill ambassadors in the history of the community.

While the K-W Symphony has emerged as the cornerstone of the local music community, with ties to a musical tradition reaching back more than a century, there are other sources of entertainment available in Kitchener. This points to the fact that—as one 1954 publication put it—"Kitchener has always been a show town."

In the early days formal concerts and theatrical productions were presented in the town hall, for lack of a more suitable venue. Performances held on less auspicious occasions were more likely to be held in a nearby barn, a large tent, or even outdoors. This continued until 1896, when Abel Walper, who founded the Walper Hotel, built the Berlin Opera House on Queen Street South. The theatre, which included a main floor and gallery, seated 600, and was the community's most modern and spacious entertainment venue to date. The first large presentation was the light opera *The Two Vagabonds,* produced by the Wilbur Opera Company.

The first lessee of the theatre was George O. "Pop" Phillip, an impresario who, according to the *K-W Record,* "brought culture to the community." A born promoter, Phillip never missed an opportunity to capitalize on a novelty. When motion pictures were first introduced in 1896, he sprang into action, advertising "The Greatest Wonder of the Age; Lumiere's Great Invention, The Cinematograph—Marvellous Motion Pictures." Movies obtained by Phillip, especially those chronicling the newsworthy events of the day, brought the people of Berlin in touch with the rest of the world. They flocked to see films of the prize fights they had read about in local newspapers and marvelled at footage of the 1906 San Francisco earthquake, Queen Victoria's diamond jubilee parade, and the coronation of King Edward VII.

The Kitchener Public Library and Doon Pioneer Park Community Centre provide numerous community services. Photo by Dave Prichard/First Light

Although Phillip loved catchy slogans, gimmicks, and novelties, he took great pride in producing high quality theatrical performances, including *Romeo and Juliet* and *Hamlet.* A professional actor himself, Phillip appreciated good theatre. But he was also a businessman, described in one local history as one of the first successful local businessmen with absolutely no knowledge of the German language.

The popularity of motion pictures eventually forced Pop Phillip's Opera House out of business in 1908. By then other theatres, like the "Theatorium," a 200-seat auditorium which opened in 1907, offered a variety of entertaining diversions, including movies. The admission price was five cents, and the patrons were treated to movies with titles like *The Butcher's Nightmare, The Spy,* and *The Horse Thief.* Of course, there was no sound, so the shows were presented with live piano accompaniment and, according to one account, a blind pianist named Metcalfe was the most popular performer. In fact, "patrons who didn't care about the movie came anyway, just to hear him turn the piano into a whole orchestra." Other theatres which operated before World War II included the Star, Roma, Allen, Imperial, Grand, and College (Century). The Capitol, with 1,000 seats, and the Lyric, with 1,200, opened in 1921. Both remain in operation, although the Capitol has subsequently been divided to create two separate theatres. The Biltmore, which became the Odeon and is now the Stages nightclub—a venue for popular rock 'n roll performers—opened in 1949.

Vaudeville, the great American stage phenomenon which spawned such legendary talents as Bob Hope, Bing Crosby, George Burns, Jack Benny, and many others, had a brief run in Kitchener. In fact, at one time four theatres featured vaudeville acts in addition to their regular movies. While the shows were by all accounts entertaining, it is doubtful if any of the future stars played in Kitchener. Vaudeville's eventual decline created a void in the area of live entertainment, and in Kitchener opened the way for live theatre, something missing since Pop Phillip's ambitious productions of Shakespeare.

Responding to this need, the K-W Little Theatre was formed to "help others realize that theatre can play an important part in their lives." Similarly, K-W Musical Productions has molded the artistic talents of many people in the area with presentations of such classics as *Fiddler on the Roof* and *West Side Story,* filling such varied locations as high school gymnasiums and the Centre in the Square.

Another local institution, the Kitchener-Waterloo Art Gallery (now located in the Centre in the Square theatre arts complex), reflects the community's enthusiasm for art—albeit an enthusiasm that was long in developing. As early as the mid-1860s, a portrait painter named Thomas Miller and a draughtsman who specialized in water-colour landscapes, S.F. Lawson, eked out meagre livings as artists in Berlin. W.H. Schmalz, an outstanding citizen who was mayor when Berlin reached city status in 1912, was a noted water-colourist. And Carl Ahrens gained a degree of international fame for his landscapes.

But in a community which took the greatest pride in its work ethic, artists were generally frowned upon as engaging in frivolity while others toiled. As was the case with the professional athletes of the era, there was something dishonourable about anyone who derived an income from what was perceived as a hobby or pleasant diversion. Although Berliners revelled in fine music, they were almost entirely unsupportive of local artists. One man changed all that by becoming one of the most acclaimed North American painters of his time and gaining fame throughout the British Empire. Born in nearby Doon in 1855, Homer Watson is undoubtedly the most important and well-known artist with whom Kitchener has ever been associated. Surprisingly, he allowed his boyhood surroundings to become a strong influence in his work even after recognizing the lack of support in the community. And he made a practice of never hiding his disenchantment with the local recalcitrants:

I wish to forget in a measure the hardship and struggle a youngster undergoes who has painting proclivities and who lives in an environment that is totally opposed to any such thing being developed . . . I could only look with dwindling admiration upon humanity as I found it in this locality . . . Humanity here was quite indifferent to any small modicum of appreciation on my part . . . They were thrifty and not artistic.

To his credit, he never stopped painting the local scenery, and soon an artistic community began to develop in his considerable shadow.

By 1880 it had become painfully obvious to anyone who looked down upon artists in general that Homer Watson was a bona fide international celebrity. In fact, he numbered among his patrons the beloved Queen Victoria, who hung one of his landscapes in Windsor Castle. As the years went by, the community was frequently abuzz with news of Watson's famous friends—noted writer Oscar Wilde, fellow artists Clausen and Whistler, and the Prime Minister of Canada, Mackenzie King. In the 1920s Watson's friend, and Group of Seven luminary, A.Y. Jackson, was frequently in Kitchener to visit his cousin, W.P. Clement. He would then meet Watson at his studio in Doon. Thanks to some generous grants from the City of Kitchener and other funding agencies, plus the support of numerous patrons, this studio has been preserved and re-

Kitchener's pioneer heritage is alluded to on the sign of local television and radio stations CKCO, CFCA-FM, and CKKW-AM. Photo by Judy-Ann Cazemier/First Light

mains a vital part of the artistic community.

In a word, Watson's impact upon the community was immense. It would not be an exaggeration to state that he single-handedly raised the awareness of art in the community to the point that people were genuinely enthusiastic about painters and painting. Ironically, the first southern Ontario exhibition of work by the internationally acclaimed Group of Seven was organized by a group of Kitchener women in 1928. Eleven paintings were purchased at the time of the show in the hope that a local art gallery could be established, but the works grew so important that they were donated to the National Gallery, where they were assured of proper care. While the people of Kitchener must now travel to Ottawa to view them, they can take justifiable pride that these irreplaceable works of art will continue to enrich the lives of all Canadians for generations to come.

When Homer Watson died in 1936, he left behind a flourishing artistic community. This renovated studio later reopened as the Doon School of Fine Art, where members of the Group of Seven frequently taught. It is quite significant that when a local art gallery was established in 1956, it was officially opened by Watson's great friend, Jackson. The first gallery, a converted bicycle shed adjacent to K-W Collegiate, was an entirely unsuitable location for the exhibition unveiled by Jackson: a collection of works by the

Oktoberfest maidens such as this one participate in Kitchener's fall festivities. Photo by Glen Jones

A lively group of Kitchener residents gathers for their city's Oktoberfest— Canada's largest Bavarian festival. Photo by Dave Prichard/First Light

This wooden Doon Village church welcomes visitors with an open door. Photo by Glen Jones

quintessential Canadian artist Tom Thomson. But the exhibition was a success, and later the art gallery obtained a permanent headquarters on Benton Street. Strangely enough, the gallery was built on the site of the birthplace of Kitchener's most famous citizen, William Lyon Mackenzie King. Today many local, regional, and national artists exhibit their work at the gallery's magnificent quarters in the Centre in the Square.

The Watson studio is not the only historical attraction of note in the community. Former Prime Minister Mackenzie King's home at Woodside is maintained by the Federal Government as a National Historic Site. The Joseph Schneider Haus, home of Kitchener's founder, is an award-winning example of historic restoration at its finest. The house is restored to its condition as it would have been in 1856. The museum is staffed by costumed interpreters who explain what life was like for the pioneer Mennonites. Activities at the Schneider Haus include quilting, schnitzing, and butchering bees, numerous exhibits, musical performances, and traditional Christmas celebrations.

Costumed interpreters are also on duty at Doon Heritage Crossroads, a re-created pioneer community on the outskirts of Kitchener. The setting was used during the filming of the television movie "Anne of Green Gables." Activities range from celebrations of Christmas and All Hallow's Eve to antique car meets and a Dominion Day garden party. Picnic facilities are available and visitors are invited to browse through the gift shop—many of whose products are made in the various interpretive centres.

While Kitchener's many artistic and cultural institutions owe their existence to the German culture so firmly rooted by the Mennonite pioneers, the ethnic make-up of the community has changed dramatically since the end of World War II and many cultures and heritages are now represented in the population. In 1941 people of German origin accounted for 48 percent of the population

ABOVE AND FACING PAGE: The Doon Heritage Crossroads features a recreated pioneer community on the outskirts of Kitchener. Above photo by Winston Fraser; facing page photo by Glen Jones

while people of British origin accounted for only 34.6 percent of the total. By 1971 those numbers had been completely reversed, with 45 percent having British backgrounds compared to 32.1 percent with German backgrounds. In 1941 the only other group to register above 5 percent were the Poles, while in 1971 it was the French. In the late 1980s people of British origin remained the largest ethnic group in the community, but many smaller groups from very different parts of the world were beginning to have an impact.

After World War II people of Asian and Mediterranean origin settled in Kitchener in greater numbers. The numbers of Italians, Greeks, and Portuguese increased significantly. Ugandans began to arrive in Kitchener in 1972, shortly after dictator Idi Amin began his bloody reign of terror. Within 10 years they numbered close to 1,000. According to the 1976 census, there were at least 25 different ethnic groups represented in the city, contrasted with 1971, when there had been only 15 groups with measurable populations. Today the most commonly heard languages other than English are German, Polish, Greek, Portuguese, French, and Croatian.

In an interesting footnote, representatives of the Cyprus Brotherhood Association believe that Kitchener's growing Cypriot population is a result of the community's namesake, Lord Kitchener, spending an important part of his career in Cyprus. He was stationed there as naval officer between 1874 and 1882. His name has remained a link with the island for many Cypriot immigrants to Canada. And that's why they come to Kitchener.

In 1967, Canada's centennial year, the K-W Regional Folk Arts Council was formed as an umbrella organization through which local ethnic communities could participate in the national centennial celebrations. The organization was such a success that ethnic leaders resolved to make it a local institution after the centennial year. Since 1973 the council, which established a Multicultural Centre, has served as a liaison between ethnic groups and the general public, government offices, educational and health services, and social and judicial offices. Its mandate is to provide a climate for broader understanding among citizens of the region.

The Multicultural Centre and Folk Arts Council sponsor the annual Canada Day celebration in Victoria Park. Arts, crafts, home cooking, and ethnic dances create an atmosphere of tolerance and acceptance.

New citizens are encouraged to participate in community events where their backgrounds are showcased. On Canada Day it is not uncommon to see a Palestinian in full Bedouin garb, Sikhs in brightly coloured turbans, and, of course, Germans in dirndls and lederhosen.

When it comes to cultural activities in Kitchener, however, nothing tops the largest Bavarian festival in Canada, Oktoberfest. Begun in 1969, the festival has gained worldwide fame. Tens of thousands of visitors flock to the Twin Cities for the 10-day event, bringing almost $10 million into the local economy. Local hotels are filled, the streets are abuzz, and the smell of sausage and schnitzel fills the air. Visitors and citizens alike enjoy everything from antique shows to barrel races, golf tournaments, archery contests, air shows, operettas, horse shows, and the nationally televised Oktoberfest Thanksgiving Day Parade.

The general manager of K-W Oktoberfest, Inc., Bill Stewart, says the goal of the festival is to "provide first-class family entertainment." This is ensured by the hundreds of Oktoberfest volunteers, who devote thousands of hours each year to ensure the success of the event. Over 20 festhalls also operate for those who prefer polkas, pretzels, and beer. Each hall devotes one day during the festival to families just to ensure that nobody gets left out of the fun. Mention Kitchener in another province, or in the U.S., and people are bound to say, "Oh yes, Oktoberfest!"

The Kitchener of 1991 is a far different place than the Kitchener of 1871—a community proud of its German heritage but not overwhelmed by it. The Oktoberfest festival is a clear example. In the festhalls and cultural venues, people of all creeds and colours gather to celebrate the heritage of their community. They know that the strength of the city lies in its tolerance and acceptance of everyone. They understand that the Oktoberfest celebration is really a reaffirmation of this strength—that Kitchener, a city born into an atmosphere of intolerance, will go to any length to ensure that every person, regardless of their background, feels welcome. But most of all, they realize that Kitchener's diversity—both ethnic and cultural—will be a key to its success in the future.

Kitchener's people are active people. Whether at work or at play, they exude an uncommon confidence in their ability to succeed. After all, the community was founded on the premise that hard work reaps the best rewards. So naturally, when it comes to sports and recreational activities, the energy level of the participants remains high. It has become a local source of pride that leisure pursuits are approached with a high level of enthusiasm and vigour.

Kitchener's renowned enjoyment of athletic and recreational endeavours was born with the community itself, and is rooted in such things as the German Sangerfeste, horse races, and various "Olympic style" competitions like bicycle, running, and swimming races. The people of Busy Berlin wanted and needed a diversion from their business concerns and became eager participants in many leisure activities.

This dedication to sports and leisure has left a remarkable legacy. It has not only enhanced the health and well-being of many generations, but it has also led to the establishment of a first-rate municipal

6 Taking Time Off

Kitchener abounds with myriad opportunities for recreation and relaxation. Photo by Glen Jones

parks system, a public-spirited municipal Department of Parks and Recreation, and numerous clubs, organized teams, and individual competitors so successful that Kitchener rightfully claims the title, "Home of Champions."

Certain sports have been dominant in different eras. Surprisingly, soccer was a major attraction in the 1880s and 1890s.

In 1880 Berlin High School principal David Forsyth convinced other soccer afficionados to form the Western Football Association. Not surprisingly, his Berlin High School team was immediately dominant, winning the first three championships. This changed in 1884, when a town team, the colourful Berlin Rangers, was formed.

The Rangers were the community's first true champions, winning the title seven times between 1885 and 1900. But competition remained the keenest at the high-school level, where Forsyth's team and the Catholic boys from St. Jerome's developed a fierce rivalry. One account describes how James E. Day of St. Jerome's and William Lyon Mackenzie King of BHS started a rather nasty brawl. (King, of course, became famous for winning brawls of the verbal kind in the House of Commons.)

Football was seen as a means of building character in young men. Historian W.V. Uttley, one of the sport's most vociferous promoters—and a noted Ranger player—summed this feeling up when he noted, "Footballers generally succeeded in life and a number gained renown." Eventually the increasing popularity of hockey and baseball relegated soccer to the background of the sporting scene, where it remained for many years.

Today the multi-cultural nature of the community has encouraged the sport's revitalization. Soccer is the most popular sport in the world and has almost become a way of life in many European and Mediterranean countries. People from these countries now living in Kitchener have established numerous teams, and have incorporated some of the pageantry of overseas soccer into the local scene. The game is thriving as never before. In the summer of 1990 the new Canadian Soccer League began play. Kitchener was granted a franchise, and the team was christened the Spirit. Playing at a renovated Centennial Stadium, the Spirit

Kitchener celebrated Canada's centennial in grand style with the construction of Centennial Stadium in 1967. Photo by Winston Fraser

The international sport of soccer has found eager participants in Kitchener's multicultural community. Photo by Dave Prichard/ First Light

attracts large and enthusiastic crowds to games against the likes of the Edmonton Brickmen and the Hamilton Steelers. The success of the Spirit is a reflection of the type of support the community traditionally gives its sports teams.

Another popular sport in the 1880s was lawn bowling. But the fact that the sport was played at a slower pace by older citizens didn't mean a low level of competition. In 1909 a rink from the Berlin Lawn Bowling Club won the Ontario Championship. The victorious foursome was skipped by future Minister of Trade and Commerce W.D. Euler. The win was greeted with a wave of celebration. According to one historian, "the Twin City gave the victors a public reception with band music and dined them at the Walper House." Euler repeated the feat in 1913, then went on to win the Dominion Championship for good measure. Lawn bowling remains popular at the Rockway Golf Club, where summer evenings are filled with laughter, whispered strategies, and good-natured jibes—a charming link with the city's sporting past.

Golf, a close cousin of lawn bowling, became popular in Berlin around the turn of the century. The first club, however, was not organized until September 1909, when a group of prominent citizens met to discuss building a course along the Grand River near Bridgeport. For $40,000 they purchased the former Hamel farm and built a clubhouse overlooking nine holes, calling it the Grand River Country Club. The club was closed in 1966 and bulldozed to make way for the Conestoga Parkway. For years the ghostly outlines of tees and greens were visible from the highway. Today the remainder of the land is occupied by industrial complexes.

In 1929 a group of members met to discuss forming a more exclusive golf club. They purchased a tract of land straddling the Kitchener-Waterloo border, hired golf course architect Stanley Thompson to create something out of the swampy bush, and in 1931 emerged with what has become one of Canada's best

The Doon Valley Golf Club is one of several local clubs providing a lovely, serene setting for residents to test their golfing skills. Photo by Dave Prichard/First Light

courses, Westmount Golf and Country Club. Curling and tennis facilities have since been added.

Rockway Golf Club had a less auspicious start. In 1932 city engineer Stanley Shupe was asked to devise a plan for the disposal of the city's outdated 124-acre Mill Street sewer farm. The Great Depression was at its height, and Shupe proposed turning the land into a golf course as a make-work project for unemployed workers. He reasoned that post-Depression Kitchener would need a municipal golf club with an open membership. A nine hole course was built in 1935 at a cost of $80,000. The first foursome to tee off included hockey greats Bobby Bauer and Woody Dumart. Later the course was expanded to 18 holes.

As a municipal golf club, Rockway attracted many golf enthusiasts who could not afford to join private clubs. Naturally, many youngsters took advantage of the facilities, and Kitchener was soon a hotbed of amateur golf. It has remained so into the present. Rockway billed itself as the "Home of Champions" because of its association with three golfers: Murray "Moe" Norman,

Gerry Kesselring, and Gary Cowan.

Moe Norman—in golf circles, the mere mention of the name brings a smile to the face. Everyone has a Moe Norman story to tell. Famous for such stunts as driving a ball using a pop bottle for a tee, Norman quickly gained a number of nicknames, ranging from "Clown Prince of Golf" to "Moe the Schmoe" and "The Magnificent Ragamuffin." But it was his skill as a golfer which truly shone. He is regarded by many experts as one of the greatest "strikers of the ball" who ever lived. He won the Canadian Amateur Championship twice, holds 32 course records across North America (including an incredible score of 59 at Rockway), and has won every major professional tournament in the country with the exception of the Canadian Open.

Golfers exercise thier skill on the Doon Valley links. Photo by Dave Prichard/ First Light

Gerry Kesselring won the Canadian Junior Championship twice, the Ontario Open four times, and the Ontario Amateur four times. He became a professional on the U.S. tour in the 1950s but returned home and regained his amateur status in the 1960s. He continues to play well in local amateur events.

While Norman and Kesselring remain truly great golfers, few athletes in the history of Canada have had as great an impact upon their community as Gary Cowan. Cowan's feats inspired an entire generation of local golfers to take up the game. His abilities first gained national attention when he won the 1956 Canadian Junior Championship. In 1961 he won the Canadian Amateur, and in 1966 he defeated the current American PGA Tour Commissioner Deane Beman in a playoff to win the United States Amateur Championship. He was only the second Canadian to win the title. That year he was named Ontario Athlete of the Year, defeating hockey superstar Bobby Hull in the voting. *Golf Digest* magazine named him top amateur golfer in the Americas.

In 1971 Cowan accomplished the unthinkable. He holed a spectacular nine iron from the rough to score an eagle and win his second U.S. Amateur—on the last hole of competition. At the end of the year, *Golf Digest* again made Cowan the highest ranked amateur on the continent. He resisted the tremendous community pressure upon him to become a professional and today is a successful insurance salesman. A member of the Royal Canadian Golf Association Hall of Fame, he has won the Ontario Amateur Championship an unprecedented 10 times and continues to be a highly ranked player.

The exploits of Norman, Kesselring, and Cowan put Kitchener at the centre of the golfing map in Canada. But with only three local courses in the early 1960s, there was little opportunity for the sport to grow. In 1966 the City of Kitchener moved to rectify the situation by purchasing the 233-acre Doon Valley Golf Club for $340,000. The club had been built in 1955 by Arnold Elmslie. The cost was partially offset when adjoining land was sold as a site for Conestoga Community College. Since then, golf courses have been established in many nearby locations. In fact, there are no less than 15 courses within a few minutes' drive from downtown Kitchener. In 1992 an exclusive new course, the Deer Ridge Country Club, will open along the banks of the Grand River between Kitchener and Cambridge, near the Pioneer Tower historic site.

Kitchener is also known as the home of numerous hockey legends—many of whom have been inducted into the National Hockey League Hall of Fame.

The first ice hockey game in which Berliners challenged a team from another city took place in Stratford, Ontario, in 1892. Perhaps because the Berliners trounced the home team by a score of 15-5, the *Stratford Herald* had nothing good to say about the exhibition:

Hockey is a polite name for bankers' shinny . . . there's no fun outside of a keg of lager, a ring of sausage and a few pretzels. A rink of curlers tried to curl while the game was on . . . In the meantime a string of bald-heads were mounted on the guarding, yelling like schoolboys or whooping like Sioux Indians.

Despite the scathing review, hockey was an instant success in the community. In 1897 a team from Berlin won the Ontario Intermediate Hockey Championship. A player on that team, Dr. John L. Gibson, eventually organized the first professional hockey league in North America—consisting entirely of teams from Ontario and Michigan. His contributions to the game were recognized with his induction into the Hockey Hall of Fame.

In 1906 the Berlin team won the Ontario Hockey Association Senior Championship, and four years later challenged the famed Montreal Wanderers for the Stanley Cup. Berlin had won the Ontario Professional League Championship while the Wanderers were champions of the fledgling National Hockey Association. In those days any successful team with enough money could challenge the cup holder. The game was played in Montreal before 3,000 fans. Berlin lost 7-3, but the town was consumed by hockey fever.

The 1950s were the golden years of amateur hockey in Kitchener. In 1953 the K-W Dutchmen won the Allan Cup, symbol of Canada's national senior hockey championship. It was the first time in 35 years that a Kitchener team had won the coveted trophy and the headline in the K-W Record reflected the city's excitement: "Twin City Goes Wild as Dutchmen Win Cup."

The team repeated the feat in 1955 and was chosen as Canada's representative to the 1956 Winter Olympics at Cortina, Italy. The local post office honoured the team by validating letters with the stamp "Home of Canada's Olympic Hockey team." In one of the most stunning upsets in hockey history, the United States—hardly a superpower on the ice—defeated the "Dutchies" 4-1. The Dutchmen also lost to the Soviet Union—then an emerging force in world hockey. Thoroughly frustrated, the team demonstrated its overwhelming power in a 23-0 destruction of the Austrian team, drawing thunderous criticism from the world press. The Dutchmen finally settled for a disappointing bronze medal.

The Dutchmen were again selected to represent Canada at the 1960 Winter Olympics in Squaw Valley, California. This time the team disposed of the Soviets, but in the original "Miracle on Ice" the United States again stunned the world, defeating the Dutchmen 2-1 to win the gold medal. The Dutchmen earned a silver medal, small consolation for a team considered to be the best in the world.

Following the Olympics, interest in senior hockey waned and the Dutchmen disbanded. The Kitchener Beavers, a professional minor league team affiliated with the New York Rangers, filled the void for several years. Ironically, Jack McCarten, the American goalie responsible for the demise of the Dutchmen in the Olympics, was drafted by the Rangers and subsequently sent to the team's Kitchener affiliate. Today the Dutchmen name is carried by the city's entry in the Mid-Western Ontario Junior B league.

In the early 1960s Junior A hockey gained a great deal of support in Kitchener. Hockey fans felt that the city needed an amateur team to replace the Dutchmen, and in 1962 Guelph's Ontario Hockey Association franchise moved to town. Under a sponsorship arrangement with the National Hockey League, the new Kitchener Rangers became an affiliate of the New York Rangers.

The Kitchener Rangers won the city's first Ontario Junior A title in 1981. Over 7,000 fans jammed a sweltering Kitchener Auditorium to witness the historic event. The following evening the *K-W Record* proclaimed, "We Are The Champions," in a typeface usually reserved for declarations of war and presidential assassinations. The hoopla and hockey fever that gripped the city was reminis-

A group of local youngsters prepares for the next play during a game of flag football. Photo by Dave Prichard/ First Light

cent of the glory days of the Dutchmen. The storybook season came to an abrupt end, however, when the Cornwall Royals defeated the Rangers 5-2 to win the Memorial Cup and the Canadian Junior Hockey Championship.

In 1982 the team again won the league title and went onto win the Memorial Cup, defeating the Sherbrooke Beavers 7-4. News of the victory set off a wild celebration in the city. In 1984 the Rangers were upset in the league playoffs by the Ottawa 67s, a team they had finished ahead of in the standings and the team they had easily defeated in the 1982 OHL final. The community was in shock. But the shock was nothing compared to the jolt felt when the same Ottawa team defeated the Rangers to win the Memorial Cup—before a hushed standing-room-only crowd at the Kitchener Auditorium.

Many former Rangers have gone on to greater things in the NHL. Some, like Paul Coffey (Edmonton, Pittsburgh), Paul Reinhart (Calgary, Vancouver), Bill Barber (Philadelphia), and Larry Robinson (Montreal, Los Angeles) are listed among the great players of the last several decades. Former team captain Brian Bellows became the league's top draft choice, and Al MacInnis won the Conn Smythe Trophy as the most valuable player in the 1989 NHL playoffs.

Today the Kitchener Rangers are a local institution. The team has remained at or near the top of the standings and the team's supporters are among the most dedicated in Canada. The traditional Friday-night games are a gathering place for the sporting community, and big games generate just as much interest as they did when senior hockey was the only game in town. It is not uncommon for a crowd of over 5,000 to jam the auditorium for a midseason game. It's a great place for families to gather, whether to watch the players on the ice or the other people in the stands. A Kitchener Ranger game is a community event, and the auditorium is an exciting place to be.

Of course, the Rangers are not the community's sole source when it comes to the production of hockey legends. Oliver L. Seibert was one of the first Canadians to play hockey on artificial ice and was the first Berliner to become a professional. His son, Earl W. Seibert, played 15 1/2 seasons in the NHL and was named to 10 consecutive all-star teams. Hughie Lehman and Albert "Babe" Siebert played in the community in the first decades of the century. Siebert had been hired to coach the Montreal Canadiens in 1939 but drowned in Lake Huron before his coaching career began. George Hainsworth, the great Montreal Canadiens goaltender, won the Vezina Trophy as the league's top goalie the first three years it was awarded. His record of 22 shutouts in 44 games during the 1928-29 season is an accomplishment almost impossible to believe in light of today's freewheeling game. Most modern goalies are lucky to record half that many shutouts in an entire career. He became a Kitchener alderman before he was killed in a 1950 automobile accident. In reporting the incident, the *London Free Press* noted, "Fate finally slipped one past George Hainsworth." All of these players are enshrined in the Hockey Hall of Fame.

Frank J. Selke, for so long the dean of NHL executives, was a Berlin native. For 20 years he was Conn Smythe's assistant with the Toronto Maple Leafs.

During that time he won three Stanley Cups. He resigned his position over philosophical differences with Smythe and took over as general manager of the archrival Montreal Canadiens. During his 18 years at the helm of the "Bleu, Blanc et Rouge," the team won six Stanley Cups, including the now legendary string of five in a row. Today the NHL presents the Frank J. Selke Trophy to the league's best defensive forward. He too is in the Hall of Fame.

Perhaps the best known of Kitchener's sports champions were hockey stars Bobby Bauer, Milt Schmidt, and Woodrow "Porky" Dumart. Together they formed the most famous forward line in NHL history—the Kraut Line. From the late 1930s to the early 1950s, they were the talk of the

Launching a hot-air balloon appears to be a labour-intensive task for these Kitchener residents. Photo by Dave Prichard/ First Light

town. They led the Boston Bruins to Stanley Cup honours in 1938-39 and 1941-42. During World War II they were known as the Kitchener Kids because their team and the NHL hierarchy felt that their German nickname reflected poorly upon the league. Those old enough to remember the Kaiser's statue being thrown into the lake at Victoria Park and the changing of the city's name from Berlin to Kitchener understood completely—they had seen it all before. But the league's edict didn't stop people from referring to them as "the Krauts." The country—and the community—had changed a great deal since 1916.

The most famous of the three was Milt Schmidt. He won the scoring title in 1939-40 and won the Hart Trophy as the league's Most Valuable Player in 1951-52. He went on to coach the Bruins and eventually became the team's general manager. He was responsible for bringing a young star named Bobby Orr into the league as an underaged junior. Many experts regard Orr as the greatest hockey player ever.

Kitchener was also well-known as the home of NHL referee Frank Udvari. He refereed in the league for 15 years and eventually became supervisor of officials. He was also a participant in one of the most bizarre incidents in hockey history. It was widely known that there was no love lost between Udvari and Canadiens legend Maurice "Rocket" Richard. Their feud came to a head when Udvari penalized the star player for a nasty incident on the ice involving the swinging of sticks. At the time Richard was closing in on the scoring title, and the suspension handed down by NHL president Clarence Campbell ruined his chances.

Although many blamed Udvari for the incident, the people of Montreal took their frustrations out on Campbell. As he took his seat in the Forum on March 17, 1955, to watch a game, the crowd turned unruly. A smoke bomb went off, rotten tomatoes were thrown, and the president was beaten. The riot spilled out into the street where rocks were thrown, shops vandalized, and automobiles burned. The incident—which all stemmed from Udvari's controversial call—

Victoria Park, the oldest of Kitchener's parks, offers a wealth of recreational opportunities for young and old alike. Photo by Dave Prichard/First Light

gained international attention. During the suspension Richard's teammate, Bernie "Boom Boom" Geoffrion, passed him and won the scoring title, further infuriating Richard's fans. Despite the "Richard Riot," Udvari is regarded as the finest official in league history, and is in the Hall of Fame as a result.

Although hockey remains Kitchener's main sporting preoccupation during the winter months, two other sports, curling and skiing, attract large numbers of participants each year. Curling dates back to the earliest days of the community when the Scots of Galt and Ayr—dominant curling communities—would come to town to challenge the Germans. A club was not formed until 1927, however, when the Kitchener and Waterloo Athletic Association raised the money to build a clubhouse. The ice was all natural, and as always, play was dictated by the whims of the weather. No women were allowed to participate for over two decades.

Artificial ice was introduced in 1928, and badminton facilities were added in 1931. In 1939 the Granite Club gained national attention when Bert Hall's rink won the Macdonald Brier Tankard (now the Labatt Brier Tankard), symbolic of the Canadian curling championship. The Granite Club was the home club of every Ontario entry in the Brier from 1938 to 1941. But Hall's triumph was the only breakthrough.

On Mother's Day 1955 much of the Granite Club was destroyed by fire. Quickly rebuilt, it remains a leading sports and social meeting place. With over 1,000 members, the Granite Club plays host to many community events and is

home base for the Kitchener Sports Association, a group of sports boosters dedicated to the promotion of sporting excellence in Kitchener.

What is now the Chicopee Ski Club was first organized in 1934. The facility was an instant hit. Over 200 members joined at $2.50 per person. The next year, a 35-metre ski jump was opened.

The ski club remained relatively unchanged for many years. The hilly terrain was eventually acquired from private owners by the Grand River Conservation Authority. Man-made snow, a staple of skiing in Southern Ontario, was first used at Chicopee in 1966. Two years later the club could boast of having 1,778 members at an annual membership fee of $35. Today annual membership runs around the 5,000 mark, making Chicopee one of the largest ski clubs in Ontario despite its modest 200-foot vertical drop. There are 12 runs, including four defined as intermediate and two as difficult. Open seven days a week, the club offers night skiing from Monday to Saturday. One triple chair, one double chair, and several T-bars carry 8,000 skiers an hour to the top of the hill. The club is one of the city's favorite winter leisure venues and is currently working on a program to expand its facilities by adding more runs and lift facilities.

Baseball and softball have also left their mark upon the community. While baseball first became popular in the 1880s, it was not until the founding of the Inter-County Baseball League in 1919 that the sport reached a sophisticated level of organization. Kitchener teams have done well at both the junior and senior levels since then, winning championships on several occasions. Today the Kitchener Panthers play at Jack Couch Park, a baseball stadium which is a part of the Centennial Stadium complex. The park was named for a long-time player, coach, executive, and booster of amateur baseball in Kitchener. The Panthers are a traditionally strong team and usually contend for the league championship.

Sportsworld, which opened in 1983, features a miniature golf course, water slide, indoor driving range, batting cages, bumper boats, and more. Photo by Winston Fraser

A father encourages his young daughter to give the slide a try. Photo by Dave Prichard/First Light

The Kitchener Kieswetters, a senior women's softball team, have put Kitchener on the national softball map. The team has won several Canadian championships since 1971 and has generated tremendous interest in the game. A fringe sport before the Kieswetters' rise to prominence, softball has become a favorite summer pastime for men and women alike. The Kieswetters play most of their games at historic Woodside Park. Today softball and slowpitch are tremendously popular recreation activities. Men, women, and children of all ages don ball gloves and head for local sports fields on summer evenings.

Many young men and women in Kitchener received their first athletic training at the local YMCA. The local "Y" had its beginnings in 1895 when a group of Berlin's most prominent citizens met to establish a branch of the successful English institution. Due to a severe lack of funds, however, it was forced to discontinue its services in 1906. From then until 1919, when A.R. Kaufman convened a meeting to re-establish the club, there was no YMCA. A timely $20,000 donation from the Breithaupt Leather Company allowed the group to purchase land at the corner of Queen and Weber streets, and a $245,000 building was subsequently constructed. Jacob Kaufman, A.R.'s father, donated $25,000 to the fund. (A.R. Kaufman's considerable contribution to the local YMCA was recognized many years later when the Y's state-of-the-art athletic/community complex was named in his memory.)

The governor general, Viscount Byng of Vimy, officially opened the new facility in 1922. Although programs for young women were not offered until the 1970s, they were allowed access to the new pool—forcing the young men to swim with their suits on, something they had never had reason to worry about before. A $750,000 renovation was completed in 1948 amid cries that the facility was far too large. In re-dedicating the building, the lieutenant governor of Ontario, L.O. Briethaupt—a Kitchener native—calmed the controversy in noting how the local YMCA had "influenced the lives of many a young gaffer, myself included."

Although the building was again renovated and expanded in 1968, it was clear by the late 1970s that Kitchener was in dire need of a new "Y." Plans for a new building at the corner of Courtland and Carwood avenues were subsequently unveiled. In 1980 an ambitious fund-raising campaign was launched, eventually raising $1.6 million. Grants of $665,000 from the Kaufman

Foundation, $1.4 million from the Ontario Lottery Corporation, and $400,000 from the City of Kitchener helped offset the cost of the sparkling—and aptly named—A.R. Kaufman Family YMCA. No longer needed, the old Queen Street building was demolished as part of the downtown revitalization scheme to make way for a condominium and office tower. Today the YMCA offers a wide variety of family-oriented programs, ranging from swimming to aerobics, racket sports, day camps for children, fitness classes, and other leisure activities. There also are special programs for seniors and the handicapped.

The YMCA has been a constant force in the well-being of the community for decades. To its credit, it has kept abreast of changing trends and the needs of the growing community. The facility has become as more popular than it has ever been as the people of Kitchener continue looking for new ways to enhance their quality of life.

While the YMCA was, and continues to be, mostly dedicated to sporting activities, the YWCA was founded to provide a clean and safe Christian home to young women from outside of the community who worked in local offices and factories. Leisure and educational programs were established to help the women adapt to the community. Today the YWCA continues to offer programs designed to broaden the horizons of the community's young women. It also provides food and shelter for young women without homes.

Another community landmark is the Kitchener Memorial Auditorium. Built in 1950, the auditorium was needed to replace the old Queen Street Auditorium, which was destroyed by fire in 1948. The new building cost $850,000 and was considered quite large for the population it served, having a seating capacity of 7,074. Since then the building has become famous as much for its sporting success as for its versatility. It has served as a training base for

Victoria Park has provided a splendid location for many a special event. Photo by Dave Prichard/First Light

the New York Rangers, as a movie set for the Tony Curtis film *Title Shot,* and as a venue for special events, ranging from the Ice Capades to the World Wrestling Federation, rock and country music concerts, university convocations, and church services.

In January 1986 twin ice pads were opened next to the auditorium. They replaced the old auditorium annex, which for years had been a community conversation piece—the dressing rooms being located at the top of a winding and rickety wooden staircase. During the annual Central Ontario Exhibition, the auditorium and annex were used for everything from livestock shows to automobile displays. The twin pads now provide a more modern setting for the fair. The twin rinks, built at a cost of $8.9 million, feature Olympic-sized ice surfaces, a fitness centre, a running track, 10 dressing rooms, and a community room with a capacity of 500. The building is linked to the original auditorium building, which underwent a substantial renovation of its own to accommodate the changes.

The Central Ontario Exhibition, held annually at the Auditorium/Centennial Stadium site, began as a traditional fall fair. But weather played havoc with attendance year after year and organizers moved the date of the fair to early summer. Attendance did increase following this change, but in recent years consistently small crowds have left the exhibition's future uncertain.

Other forms of leisure activity are offered by two major privately operated amusement parks.

Bingeman Park was opened on the Bingeman family farm just off Victoria Street in 1960. The founders, whose main business was Kitchener Dairies, opened a lodge building on the site in 1961, and in 1964 added open-air roller skating to the park's activities. Soon requests for campsites led to construction of a campground. Today, the park's convention facilities are used year round for everything from trade shows to banquets, and the amusement facilities are packed with vacationing families during the summer months. With a water slide, wave pool, swimming pool, driving range, go-carts, bumper boats, roller skating, campgrounds, and miniature golf, there is an activity for everyone in the family.

Pioneer Sportsworld opened in July 1983. The brainchild of local businessmen Del Wideman and Don Nurse, Sportsworld features an indoor driving range and pro shop, an arcade, a gift shop, a restaurant, 36 holes of miniature golf, a water slide, batting cages, go-carts, bumper boats, a wave pool, and the well-known "Big Dipper" slide. The artificial turf used in the driving range and on the miniature golf courses is actually the old field surface from Exhibition Stadium in Toronto—the former home of Toronto's Blue Jays and Argonauts.

Kitchener is well-endowed with municipal recreational facilities. These include indoor swimming pools at the Breithaupt Community Centre and at Forest Heights and Cameron Heights collegiates. Outdoor pools operate at Idlewood, Wilson, and Woodside parks during the summer months. Besides the Memorial Auditorium complex, the winter sports of hockey and skating can be enjoyed at five arenas (Grand River, Don McLaren, Queensmount, Wilson, and Lions) as well as on the lake at Victoria Park.

Baseball, softball, and soccer are summertime fixtures at numerous parks around the city, most notably at Budd Park, a multi-purpose sports field built through the co-operation of the Province of Ontario, the City of Kitchener, and Budd Canada. The park features several lighted sports fields and a field house with dressing rooms and an adjacent refreshment stand. Its excellent conditions

The setting sun brings yet another day to a close in Kitchener. Photo by Aubrey Diem/First Light

and easy access makes it a popular venue for many local sports leagues.

Kitchener also boasts a thriving network of neighbourhood associations which look after the interests of citizens in different sections of the community. Leisure activities, ranging from bingo to card games and athletic competitions, are organized by volunteers at community centres (Breithaupt, Centreville, Chicopee, Mill Courtland, and the Victoria Park Pavilion) throughout the city. Senior citizens are invited to join in the fun at the Rockway, Charles Street, and Breithaupt seniors' centres. Some seniors use these centres as home base for small businesses they operate catering to the needs of their contemporaries. They include landscaping, woodworking, and general handyman jobs.

The Kitchener Parks and Recreation Department oversees much of the city's organized leisure activities, including highly successful minor sports programs for baseball, basketball, fastball, football, gymnastics, hockey, judo, lacrosse, girls' ringette, skating, soccer, ski racing, girls' softball, speed skating, track and field, waterpolo, and wrestling. In addition, the department is involved in the promotion of the nationally respected Region of Waterloo Swim Club, which counts among its alumni the late Olympic champion and world record holder Victor Davis. The minor sports organization is an excellent way for new families to become acquainted with the community.

With such a long history of athletic and leisure success behind it, it is hardly surprising that, in the last decade, Kitchener has gained fame as the home of super-heavyweight boxing champion and Olympic gold medallist Lennox Lewis. Lewis was the first Canadian to win the world junior boxing championship, and his masterful performance at the 1988 Seoul Olympics helped boost the spirits of a Canadian team devastated by the Ben Johnson scandal. At six feet five inches and 220 pounds, Lewis is an imposing figure, yet his sense of humour and modesty is discussed as much as his fistic prowess. Now a successful professional with sights set on the world heavyweight championship, Lennox Lewis is living proof that Kitchener's lofty perch as the "Home of Champions" will continue to inspire local athletes in the decades to come.

2

KITCHENER'S ENTERPRISES

KITCHENER'S BUSINESS AND PROFESSIONAL COMMUNITY BRINGS A WEALTH OF SERVICE, ABILITY, AND INSIGHT TO THE AREA.

7

BUSINESS AND PROFESSIONS

Photo by Judy-Ann Cazemier

THE WALTER FEDY PARTNERSHIP

J.M. Schneider Inc.

In an era of rising concern about the environment, effective energy management, and budget constraints, The Walter Fedy Partnership has accumulated an impressive array of projects of varying complexity and demands. This integrated partnership of architects and engineers thrives on the challenges facing

A.R. Kaufman Family Y.

The Mutual Group.

today's project client. Testament to its success is evidenced in the percentage of the firm's projects derived from repeat clients and referral clients.

The 70-member staff of specialists excels in the application of creative insight in all of their assignments, regardless of size or budget. A full-service integrated

team approach is brought to bear on every building challenge, ensuring a complete and coherent resolution of the client's requirements.

The company has fueled its growth with a commitment to the primary objective of quality work, on time and within budget. The success of this approach is confirmed by a rapidly growing client list of industrialists, private corporations, governments, and institutions.

How does this team of design professionals and project managers continue to bring this diverse array of projects to completion on time and on budget? The answer lies in a commitment to providing excellent service to the client. To achieve this, the client becomes an integral part of the design team from beginning to end.

The key word in this approach is "team." The assets of The Walter Fedy Partnership derived from many sources cultivated over 40 challenging years reinforce function, efficiency, and economy as the cornerstones of each project.

Transport Canada.

Conestoga Cold Storage Limited.

As the company has progressed its multi-disciplinary service has widened into all facets of architecture and from the full structural, mechanical, and electrical elements of engineering to municipal land use, cost control, and financial planning departments.

Commencing with a clear definition of the customer's goals, architectural and engineering consultants analyze problems and solutions and communicate their findings to the client. The process of mutual understanding moves through the design inventory or investigative phase of the exercise and on to the creative stage, where the project begins to take shape with the introduction of financial, site, and design solutions. Each project proceeds under the direction of a project manager supported by expertise from the other departments. Complementing this capability is a finely tuned project management division, which enables owners to professionally manage and construct their facilities, meet deadlines, and plan strategies cost effectively.

The design team's ability to

Lutheran Life Insurance Society.

respond to a changing marketplace and incorporate the best technological advances in computer-assisted design, combined with its emphasis on the skills development of personnel, ensures the client a leading edge project where nothing falls through the cracks.

The firm's portfolio includes a wealth of successful projects, from office buildings to sports and recreation complexes, from cold storage facilities to industrial process lines, and from airport control towers to police headquarters, schools, retirement homes, churches, and health care facilities—each project draws from a comprehensive inventory of previous experience.

From programming, design, contract documentation, and administration to feasibility studies, analytical engineering, and energy management, The Walter Fedy Partnership subscribes to the pursuit of excellence, not simply in the design or engineering functions of project development but in all the facets contained in the successful completion of a project of lasting value.

Johnson & Johnson/McNeil Consumer Products.

GATEMAN-MILLOY INC.

A perfectly struck drive from the first tee at Devil's Pulpit golf course will soar off toward the CN Tower, which is 30 miles to the south. The ball will land on a perfectly manicured fairway, glistening against the craggy background of the Caledon Hills, north of Brampton.

Devil's Pulpit was developed by two of the inventors of the board game Trivial Pursuit. The task of transforming 320 acres of rough Niagara Escarpment terrain into one of Canada's toughest golf courses was given to Gateman-Milloy Inc. of Kitchener.

The project is the latest major accomplishment of the decade-old alliance of Blaire Gateman and Michael J. Milloy. Gateman is a graduate of the University of Guelph; Milloy is a graduate of

Landscaping and construction of paths and retaining walls, residential complex.

Golf course construction: Devil's Pulpit, Caledon.

the Niagara Parks Commission School of Horticulture.

Their commitment to providing a superior level of client service has forged a reputation for relia-

bility and professionalism. It has also built a $25-million-a-year enterprise with 230 employees and branches in Western Canada and the United States. From its original base as a landscape contractor, the company has extended its expertise into several other related areas, particularly golf course

construction.

The company regularly undertakes major construction projects designed by leading landscape architects for major corporations and government clients and has a healthy working relationship with major general contractors and land developers.

For owners of industrial, commercial, and residential properties, Gateman-Milloy offers a professional landscape design service as part of a design/build approach. The company also provides a complete year-round, "worry free" maintenance service, which ranges from landscape design to turf care to snow removal. Maintenance clients include such well-known names as Britannica, Johnson & Johnson, and Toyota.

Similar maintenance services are provided at municipal parks and recreation facilities, but in addition to turf and hard-surface maintenance, the company also is involved in the construction of ball diamonds, soccer fields, running tracks, tennis courts, and miniature golf layouts.

Gateman-Milloy operates a large fleet of company-owned vehicles and state-of-the-art construction and maintenance equipment. The company has a 63-acre nursery at New Dundee and a 300-acre sod farm near Elora to ensure a readily available supply of plant material.

A subsidiary, Fast Forest Inc., specializes in the planting or relocating of large trees. Operating a fleet of technologically advanced tree spades, Fast Forest can readily move trees of up to 40 feet tall and up to 10 inches in trunk cal-

Construction of parks and recreational facilities.

liper. This capability is a major asset in creating "instant" landscaping by adding or moving large trees on a property. The company's expertise in building golf courses started with a relatively small municipal project in Etobicoke. It has grown with the construction of Royal Woodbine (near Pearson International Airport in Toronto) and Devil's Pulpit. In the summer of 1990, six other courses were either under construction or about to start.

Gateman-Milloy's growing reputation and capability in this highly specialized area was recognized when the company was accepted for membership in the select 27-member Golf Course Builders of America Association. From a modest beginning in 1981, Gateman-Milloy Inc. has become a major force in the landscape contracting and golf course construction industry. As the partners enter their second decade, they will continue to build their business by maintaining their commitment to quality workmanship, dependable service, and a professional approach to each project.

Large tree planting by Fast Forest subsidiary.

PARAGON ENGINEERING LIMITED

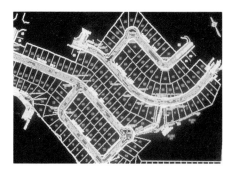

ABOVE: A Paragon Engineering land development plan.

LEFT: Paragon's corporate office in Kitchener houses its administrative and design facilities.

Paragon is the little engineering company that grew—from a quartet of founders in a single office scarcely a decade ago to a multidisciplined service of proven competence and capability.

The description fits the profile of Paragon Engineering Limited, a Kitchener-based consulting engineering firm known for personalized service, innovative solutions, and technical excellence. Very much a part of progress in and around Kitchener, the firm is also identified with a growing roster of public- and private-sector projects throughout Ontario.

From incorporation in 1979, the company has emerged as a major force in its professional sphere. Of some 120 personnel, 35 are graduate engineers. Headquarters is a spacious suite of offices and design areas in the new corporate centre at 871 Victoria Street North, with branches in Bracebridge, London, and Port Elgin. Services range from feasibility studies and environmental assessment through to final design and contract administration.

A unique and intricate project for Paragon was the engineering of Sportsworld's site services on the southern outskirts of Kitchener.

Paragon personnel represent the cornerstone of its success in the general fields of municipal, land development, water resources, and mechanical/electrical/structural engineering. A diverse staff of professional engineers, scientists, technologists, surveyors, and field crews is supported by sophisticated technical and administrative systems. A team approach led by senior engineers is enhanced by advanced resources, such as total station surveying and computer-aided design and drafting (CADD).

An accelerating rate of growth dating from 1986 has triggered assignments for most of the major land developers and builders in the region as well as a host of

large-scale projects for municipalities and large commercial enterprises. Paragon has carried out numerous road and bridge reconstructions and waterworks installations, such as part of the current Mannheim water project. It provided site-servicing design for major regional buildings, airport configurations at several Ontario cities, drainage studies for conservation authorities, and a variety of work for large corporations across Canada.

The founders of Paragon Engineering Limited remain in charge today. They are Ray Alarie, president; Mark Jackson, vice president; Jack Gorrie, vice president; and Brad Pryde, Port Elgin manager. Many newer "partners" round out the senior management team.

HALLMAN GROUP

As the foremost private apartment and development company in southwestern Ontario, the Hallman Group is comfortable with big numbers. In 46 years of diversified activity, president and owner Lyle Hallman has fashioned a mammoth residential holding in the region. And now, while still active in business, he is deriving satisfaction from recent commitments as a benefactor of the community.

Hallman Property Management, Hallman Construction, and the balance of the 15-division Hallman Group function from their office at 230 Gage Avenue in Kitchener and rely on a capable staff of three office workers, four property managers, and six maintenance workers, plus four family executives. Only when the computer churns out a listing of nearly 4,000 residential apartment units and 85 superintendents at sites in the Twin Cities, Cambridge, and several peripheral communities does the real profile emerge.

What stands today as a multimillion-dollar assembly of accommodation and commercial properties traces to Lyle Hallman's return from war service to form a construction company in 1945. A native of Preston, he started by renovating stores in downtown Kitchener, advanced to home building on a large scale in the mid-1960s, and eventually banked 1,000 acres of developable land in the area. Hallman at one point was completing more than 100 homes per year; the firm still owns 800 acres that are being released to builders in the form of serviced residential lots.

The past decade has seen increasing emphasis on apartment building, at a rate of 200 suites per year, by the Hallman Group.

Two of the many Hallman properties: 200 Shakespeare Drive (ABOVE) in Waterloo and Parkview Tower (RIGHT) at 95 Cambridge Street in Cambridge.

Presently a shopping centre at Ottawa and Lackner, which was launched with a supermarket in 1989, is being filled out with a strip mall to occupy 125,000 square feet. In all of these ventures, founder and sole owner Lyle Hallman is assisted by dedicated and capable employees, some with 35 years of service. Company officers include his wife, Wendy, senior property manager, and his sons: Peter, controller; Jim, construction supervisor; and Tom, property manager.

Over the years the Hallman organization has earned awards for building excellence from the Kitchener/Waterloo Home Builders Association, of which Lyle Hallman was a founding member in 1946 and later president, and from the Canadian Home Builders Association, where he held various offices. For most of his career, Hallman has maintained a community role, highlighted by lengthy

service to the K-W Counselling Services, a non-profit advisory to people with emotional concerns. In 1988 he made a stunning $500,000 gift to the new swimming pool in the Grand River Recreational Complex, and one year later Hallman donated an unprecedented one million dollars to the Kitchener and Waterloo Community Foundation. In each case, the monetary amounts were consistent with the generous style of the Hallman Group.

PROCTOR & REDFERN LIMITED

An enduring and vital involvement in the design and engineering of municipal services for the Kitchener/Waterloo area spans a 60-year association with one of Canada's foremost engineering companies. Over that period Proctor & Redfern Limited has specified and installed a variety of water and sewer works in the city, region, and surrounding counties. As well, the company's expertise has been applied to special situations in southwestern Ontario and, in one instance, to the Middle East.

A brick-lined tunnel outfall sewer from the Waterloo sewage treatment plant in the 1930s marked Proctor & Redfern's debut in the Twin Cities. But it was not until 1957 that a Kitchener office opened in Murray Schmitt's Maplewood Place home to oversee design and construction of the Kitchener sewage treatment plant. Soon operations were moved to the Dunker building, coincident with the transfer of many Toronto-based projects to Kitchener for better site/client proximity. Dislodged by the King Centre construction, the firm functioned at 655 King Street East for 15 years until occupying its present office on New Dundee Road in 1989.

The company's reputation on the local scene was consolidated by W.B. Redfern, a senior sanitary engineer who had joined the organization in 1919, just seven years after its founding. He proceeded to engineer water systems for Kitchener and Waterloo through the 1930s and 1940s. Commencing in 1947 Proctor & Redfern received an added dimension of recogni-

The Victoria Lake flood control outlet in Kitchener.

tion through Kitchener Panthers baseball pitcher Roy Tredgett, who was resident engineer at the Waterloo sewage plant. (Tredgett became president of the firm in 1978).

From 1940 to 1960, Proctor & Redfern Limited handled master storm sewer and trunk sanitary sewer projects in east-end Kitchener and assisted municipalities and water utilities commissions with services in Waterloo, Wellington, Perth, Grey, Bruce, and Brant counties. Major undertakings were waterworks for Kitchener, Waterloo, Preston, Hespeler, Walkerton, and Hanover; sewage treatment plants for Galt, Preston, Fergus, Brantford, Waterloo, and St. Mary's; and bridge designs for Waterloo County, Kitchener, and Fergus.

The 1960s and 1970s saw the

Kitchener office meet the challenge of storm-water management on the Schneider Creek flood control project and assist with downtown Kitchener and St. Mary's improvements. Early in the 1980s Kitchener personnel provided master planning and design of services for the new King Abdul Aziz University in Saudi Arabia.

Today the Kitchener branch is managed by Larry Mason, who succeeded Walter Robinson in 1979. The office provides a full range of engineering and planning services, including specialized counsel in computer technology, waste management, and water and wastewater technology.

Design of 120,000 m³/d Kitchener sewage treatment plant.

B&B KIESWETTER EXCAVATING INC.

Scarcely a decade into gravel supply and site contracting, an enterprising partnership of Kitchener brothers is well launched into new ventures closely associated with their core business.

B&B Kieswetter Excavating Inc. is building on a reputation for quality service dating from its first major project, Centre in the Square. That was in late 1978, just after the company was formed by co-owners Bryan and Bob Kieswetter. Since then they have managed a succession of site preparations for area builders while expanding their own field of expertise.

Recently, on the heels of its award-winning River Oaks Estates development, the firm secured Canadian rights and commenced to market a revolutionary mortar process, Mega Mix. Acceptance of the concept will add a national dimension to B&B, which is regionally well known for its sand and gravel

The Mega Mix filling station, opened in 1989.

The award-winning River Oaks Estates, developed in 1988.

operations. As a rule the company has five to 10 contract jobs drawing on a staff of 45 people and a large array of equipment deployed from headquarters at 1801 Bleams Road.

The founders, whose family has lived in the district since the 1850s, brought considerable experience to the operation at the outset. Bryan had learned the trade from his father, Walter; Bob had spent five years managing a local engineering consulting firm after graduating as a civil engineer from the University of Waterloo. In fact they represent the third generation in the gravel business, which is appropriate since the family name means "gravel weather" in German.

Start-up was a 20-acre sand and gravel property. Subsequently 75 acres was acquired at Bleams and Trussler to the west, and later on pits in North Waterloo and Baden, for a current total of 400 acres. The River Oaks project entailed conversion of an abandoned pit to 22 estate lots around Emerald and Grand lakes. The subdivision

sight lines were enhanced by tiering toward the Grand River, with all natural areas used to support fish and wildlife habitats. National publicity accompanied a Property Development Award to B&B from the Aggregate Producers Association of Ontario.

Bright orange signs of the Holland-developed Mega Mix mortar silo system reflects excitement in the Kieswetter organization today. The company is pursuing the extension of dealerships from its first filling station, which dispatches silos containing sand and cement for precision blending at construction sites in southwestern Ontario. Along with this new technology from the Dutch comes the Canadian rights to distribution of the NCH lift, which makes 25-ton truck bodies interchangeable, as well as the multi-compact system, a new technology developed to compact waste at garbage transfer stations. B&B Kieswetter Excavating Inc. is an excavator with a difference.

PRODUCING AND DISTRIBUTING GOODS FOR INDI-VIDUALS AND INDUSTRY, MANUFACTURING FIRMS PROVIDE EMPLOYMENT FOR MANY KITCHENER AREA RESIDENTS.

MANUFACTURING

Photo by Dave Prichard/
First Light

ADVANCE METAL INDUSTRIES LIMITED

ABOVE: Lyle Schneider, plant engineer, programs and sets up one of the wire electrical discharge machines. Schneider has provided the company with his engineering expertise for more than 20 years.

LEFT: Ross Gilders (left), president and founder, and his son, Barry Gilders, vice president and plant manager, discuss the engineering techniques required to tool a particular part.

A rising capability in the field of tool and die making underpins a small but progressive Kitchener company at the forefront of a select industrial group in southern Ontario.

Advance Metal Industries Limited responds to a broadening demand for custom machining from a diverse clientele right across the spectrum of North American manufacturing. Its skilled craftspeople, upgraded plant, and modern equipment represent almost a half-century of commitment by two generations of family management.

Today the flourishing business continues to function on founding principles of quality and service, but it excels on a higher technical level by access to electrical discharge machines (EDM) and computerization. With current strength of 28 employees and 19,000 square feet of shop and office space, the firm is well positioned to meet new challenges.

The present locale and profile of Advance Metal at 133 Dundas Street is several dimensions larger than the modest die-making venture launched by Ross Gilders with partner P.L. Barber in the former's home basement in 1946. A native of Hespeler, Gilders brought pre-

war experience with Dominion Electrohome to the production of dies and moulds for local firms. The business quickly became a full-time operation, with two employees and five machines. In 1950 Gilders, who continues as president, bought out Barber.

From a brief tenure in the old Kitchener Electronics building, the company moved in 1950 to rented premises in the Apex Metals (Kitchener) Limited plant on Dundas Street, where it was incorporated the following year. Also in 1951 Advance Metal built a 2,000-square-foot addition adjacent to Apex Metals and then doubled the space by 1954. In 1972, as orders increased and the staff grew to 22 people, Advance Metal bought the Apex building to bring the operating area to its present size.

has resulted in both the graduation of personnel to establish their own shops and the retention of many employees—including several with more than 20 years of service—on the plant floor of Advance Metal. Their combined expertise extends from the most minute jewellery industry dies to dies weighing in excess of 12,000 pounds for the automotive sector. Other industries served by the tradespeople, engineers, and designers in this bustling enterprise are appliance, home hardware, and farm equipment suppliers, as well as the construction and electronics spheres.

While Ross Gilders is still very active in company policy, direct responsibility for operations now rests with his son Barry, who is vice president and plant manager. Barry's wife, Sabine, is treasurer and an active part-time member of the staff. Lyle Schneider is plant engineer; Meedi Ruutopold is office manager.

All of the people at Advance Metal Industries Limited take a personal interest and pride in the craftsmanship of every assignment during its transmission through the plant. They are vigilant about the entire process, whether administration or planning; the multitude of grinders, drills, saws, lathes, milling machines, and presses; or on-time shipping and delivery. It is this attitude, according to Ross and Barry Gilders, that contributes measurably to the success of their company.

From inception, each year has seen improvements in the form of new machinery and equipment and updating of the premises. New offices were built in 1985, after which the old administrative section was fully occupied by quality control and computer-assisted design and manufacturing (CAD/CAM) systems. The EDM department facilitates mastery of a new found world of accuracy, simplicity, and repeat performance in the intricacies of tool and die making. Previously unattainable detail, shape, extrusion dies, electrodes, and an infinite variety of products flow from two conventional machines and two computer-controlled travelling wire EDM units.

Blending with the company's 45 years of experience is a strong accent on in-house training, which

ABOVE: The tool and die assembly area.

BELOW: This Keller tracing machine can duplicate in steel a wooden model of any shape up to 4 feet by 6 feet in size.

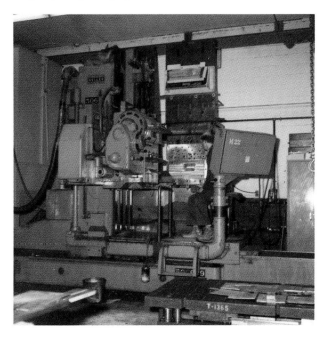

KUNTZ ELECTROPLATING INC.

National stature as an industry leader and local origins in the dawn of the Twin Cities merge in a distinctive profile at Kuntz Electroplating Inc.

The company has come a long way in time and product from nineteenth-century family roots in the brewery trade. But its high-technology metal-finishing plant in Kitchener is only a few miles from the original Waterloo site of patriarch David Kuntz's beer, cask, and brick-making operations of the 1830s.

shift shop opened by Oscar Kuntz and his son David in 1948. A garage on Princess Street near the Huether Hotel (where the first Kuntz entrepreneurs had labored a century earlier) was the first home of the electroplating venture. However, Oscar Kuntz brought back to his home city some 25 years of experience in motor-vehicle finishing with northern U.S. companies. Within four years his business was re-located to Nyberg Street in Kitchener with 48 employees and 6,000

Kuntz, brothers Robert, Paul, and Louis, and brothers-in-law Jack Karn and Bob Germann worked with Oscar Kuntz to outgrow the capacity of the Nyberg Street plant by 1965. Moving to the present location, they proceeded with another series of additions and modernizations to broaden capacity. More than 100 employees were needed in 1970, then 50 more just three years later, and soon a total of 200 workers were employed. A large and loyal clientele anchored in the vehicle, consumer goods,

Kuntz Electroplating's plant on Wilson Avenue today, where more than 400 people are employed.

Now, several generations later, another prolific branch of the family is perpetuating a tradition committed to progress—this time as the foremost open-shop electroplater in Canada. Employing more than 400 people, Kuntz Electroplating services a broad spectrum of the automotive, commercial, military, and aerospace industries on an international basis.

The firm's modern, 176,000-square-foot production facility at 851 Wilson Avenue is many dimensions larger than the make-

square feet of working area.

Multiple extensions of the plant and its specialties featured the next two decades as the Kuntz organization gained renown for excellence in the polishing and plating of household appliances, aircraft, radar components, and automobiles. While saddened by the death in 1961 of co-founder David

and aircraft sectors required a doubling of plant facility to 52,000 square feet in 1973 and to approximately half the current size in 1978. That year Kuntz Electroplating became a division of Magna International Inc.

As new quality control, laboratory, and upgraded equipment came into play, and departments were again expanded in the mid-1980s, Kuntz aspired to top ranking on the continent. Technological advances contributed to innovative solutions and cost-effective techniques in

The 1959 product line is proudly displayed by Bob Kuntz, Sr. (left, 1990 president), Oscar Kuntz (center, deceased), and Dave Kuntz (right, deceased).

response to a clientele exceeding 125 Canadian and American firms. State-of-the-art production facilities and knowledgeable personnel—many with more than 20 years of

The 1990 chrome-plated products.

service—continue to maintain Kuntz as the number one plater in North America.

A partial list of coatings serves to illustrate this capability, which is subject to rigorous inspection and testing all down the production lines. The company is

equally competent in the provision of copper, duplex and triplex nickel, chrome plating (on steel and aluminum), zinc plating (black, olive drab, yellow, and bright chromates), phosphating (zinc and manganese), electroless nickel and nickel composites, hard-chrome plating, passivation of stainless steel, and anodizing of aluminum. Kuntz Electroplating will also consolidate its position in the marketplace of the 1990s by adaptation to new products and finishes through laboratory testing, sampling, and by rigorous quality-assurance procedures.

The firm's dedication to in-plant efficiency and client satisfaction was restated by president Robert Kuntz and secretary/treasurer Paul Kuntz on January 31, 1990, when they bought back Magna International's 60 percent interest in Kuntz Electroplating Inc. to hold total ownership. In fact, the 12-year relationship with Magna was notable for an autonomous, well-run operation at Kitchener, emerging as a strong company in all aspects. The owners, who have been joined by a sixth generation of the Kuntz family actively participating in the business, stand committed to a high standard of product and service.

WESTON BAKERIES

Significant contributions to the local economy and community betterment and an integral role in Weston Bakeries' continental leadership have accompanied the growth of the Kitchener division during the past 45 years.

Supported by the parent Weston Foods organization and guided by skilled management, the production/distribution personnel associated with the modern city facility have built a broad base of patronage in southwestern Ontario. From the initiatives of early general managers to greatly increased capacity today, the Kitchener plant has evolved into a state-of-the-art bakery with a reputation for quality and consistency. Its payroll is valued by the community, just as the various interests of company and employees are appreciated by area residents.

The inception of the present Weston establishment on Victoria Street North took place in another century on another Twin Cities site—in January 1899 at 19 Foundry Street (now Ontario Street). There Henry A. Dietrich applied a talent for fresh-baked bread that by 1917 was selling at a rate of one million loaves annually. When Garfield Weston purchased the business in September, 1946, annual sales were more than $100,000 from what was then the leading supplier of breads, cakes, cookies, and pies, with 11 delivery routes in the district.

Weston administration commenced to outstrip those num-

bers with construction of the first 50,000 square feet of the present plant. Opened in June 1948, the plant produced 80 varieties of bread, buns, and cakes. Within a year of occupying the new $415,000 bakery, sales exceeded $1.2 million from production led by 7.6 million loaves in 1949. Under the direction of the first general manager, Norman Brenner, the plant soon surpassed 100,000 pounds of baked goods weekly. Throughout the tenure of succeeding managers—V.G. Ursaki, F.B. Osborne, R.M. Hincks, R.J. Bow-

Henry A. Dietrich (far left) poses with three of his bakers in the oven room of Dietrich's Bakery. Courtesy, Waterloo Historical Society

man, G.A. Ellig, and J.D. Hagerman (1990)—the upward trend has continued.

Expansions also occurred at frequent intervals. An office and dock addition in 1960 was followed by a freezer storage in 1979; lockers, lunch rooms, and another freezer in 1980; office and plant extensions in 1981-1984; and a shipping room

One million pounds of baked goods are produced in Kitchener each week. This includes such nutritious branded breads as Wonder®, County Harvest®, Fibre Goodness®, and Stonehouse Farm®.

After undergoing numerous expansions, today the Weston plant in Kitchener covers more than 135,000 square feet. The facilities include a garage, body shop, thrift store, and sales offices in addition to the state-of-the-art bakery.

expansion in 1989. Now the plant covers more than 135,000 square feet and produces bread, rolls, sweet goods, English muffins, and some frozen dough products. A garage, body shop, thrift store, and sales office are maintained in Kitchener, which services branches in Brantford, London, Walkerton, and Chatham and a total of 92 routes. Today the Kitchener ovens and ancillary equipment turn out in excess of one million pounds of goods a week. Its 500 employees function in a much larger and more efficient environment, but they retain an historic link—the Dietrich name is on the majority of the whole-wheat lines.

The Kitchener division has supported numerous causes in the region over the years, ranging from participation in the Mennonite world relief drive to sponsorship of the Shrine Circus in 1990 as part of a national Weston program. Company and staff also contributed to the YMCA and YWCA building funds, Big Sisters, Junior Achievement, and the K-W Symphony, to name a few. The division also operates surplus or thrift stores that sell some products at below-retail prices, and the division further discounts goods for a number of community purposes.

The Kitchener plant is a high-performing unit of Weston Bakeries, which in turn is a part of Weston Foods, one of three principal operating groups (the others are Loblaw Companies and Weston Resources) comprising George Weston Limited. This Canadian company conducts food processing and distribution and forest and fisheries businesses throughout Canada and the United States with a combined annual sales volume approaching $11 billion.

Modernizations and expansions at Kitchener over the years are consistent with long-term advancement in the baking division. From flour mills to finished product, the people at Weston have responded to a host of market changes as a pacesetter in the food industry. Now the company is again setting trends as consumer preferences splinter in every possible direction: diet and indulgence, nutrition and taste, convenience and variety, family size and single portion, easy to use and environmentally friendly.

In nutrition alone, Weston is pursuing a very strong program under the banner of "nutrition focus" based on the health appeal of bread. Commencing in 1988, new nutritional labelling guidelines led to promotion of bread as low in fat and devoid of cholesterol. Subsequently, Weston Bakeries commenced to lead the industry in a nutrition awareness front that is ongoing both publicly and in house.

Weston Bakeries is also committed to objectives of a non-financial nature that have been in place for some time but were formalized in 1989 by a resource, environmental, and waste management policy. Managers have commenced to implement these practices in support of a corporate determination "to leave a lighter footprint on planet earth." In addition, the company is continuing to assist organizations involved in medical research, education, and community aid to the less advantaged.

Weston Bakeries retains the Dietrich's® name on several very popular whole-wheat breads.

BONNIE STUART SHOES LIMITED

Craftsmanship, specialization, and an historic presence form a solid foundation for the oldest and one of the most successful children's shoe manufacturers in Canada. Bonnie Stuart Shoes Limited is a progressive, family-owned enterprise with 80 years experience in a select field, a nationally known brand name, and few equals on the continent among a handful of survivors in a fiercely competitive business. Management shares with 80 employees a dedication to foot health and access to the latest industry technology within a well-equipped, 23,000-square-foot plant at 141 Whitney Place in Kitchener.

The company was organized in 1910 by Dr. J.H. Radford and his son-in-law A.M. Stuart. It was incorporated on May 1, 1911, as the Galt Shoe Company on Water Street in what is now downtown Cambridge. Dr. Radford continued as president until 1936, but Stuart ran the firm, which was recognized for excellence of product by the Shoe Manufacturers Association of Canada. Stuart's son Andy, who succeeded as president in 1946, is a past director of the Footwear and Leather Institute of Canada. The third generation is represented by Cameron Stuart, vice president and general manager. The other shareholder is secretary/treasurer David McCallum.

From the beginning, the Stuarts excelled in the design and fitting of children's shoes. Their expertise was transferred to Kitchener in 1924 as the result of a fire that destroyed the five-storey Galt building. Andy

Bonnie Stuart is the oldest and one of the two most successful children's shoe manufacturers in Canada.

Stuart, then four years old, remembers the blackened site identified by only a steel vault sticking out of the ground. With an insurance settlement of $77,640, management opted for a Kitchener location due to better rail service— of vital importance in that era. Rented premises on Brei-

thaupt Street in the old Canada Trunk and Bag building, and then the York Trading structure on King Street, led to the first company-owned plant at the present one-acre site in 1953.

It was there that Andy Stuart imprinted his stamp in 1959 with adoption of the familiar tartan lids and Scottish terrier logo associated with the change of name to Bonnie Stuart. He also ventured into national advertising to promote the company across Canada, an advancement paying dividends decades later from annual production of some 250,000 pairs of shoes.

The future of this thriving company is further ensured by involvement in research, seminars, and conferences devoted to orthopedic footwear, such as the Canadian Prescription Footwear Association. This serious approach to fitting children's shoes— and a special men's orthopedic line—is supported by self-sufficiency through staff training and a large investment in computer-assisted pattern making and stitching within the Bonnie Stuart Shoes Limited facility.

Bonnie Stuart Shoes Limited moved into its present one-acre facility in 1953. Since that date two additions have been made onto the building (photo taken in 1963, following first addition).

Photo by Dave Prichard

**KITCHENER'S RETAIL PRODUCTS AND SERVICE IN-
DUSTRIES PROVIDE THE COMMUNITY WITH A BET-
TER STANDARD OF LIVING.**

PRODUCTS AND SERVICES

*Photo by Dave Prichard/
First Light*

KITCHENER UTILITIES

A unique, historic, and progressive public utility meets the basic daily requirements of more than 40,000 residential and commercial customers in the city.

Kitchener Utilities fulfils a dual role in distributing for its customers both natural gas and water. Both are vital commodities that home owners and businesses alike count on being there at the push of a button or turn of a tap. The supply of such fundamental products to some 30,000 gas and 40,000 water consumers is handled efficiently by the 60 people employed by the utility.

The local experience with these fundamental products traces back well over a century to private sources in the community then known as Berlin. From an early transition to public ownership

Clean, safe, efficient natural gas.

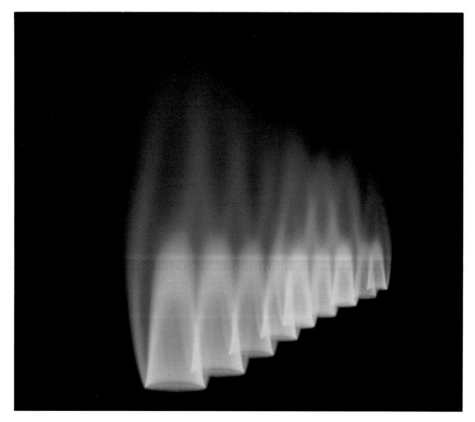

and subsequent growth and modernization, Kitchener Utilities has claimed a special place amid a rich cultural heritage. Today it stands as the only city-owned and city-operated natural-gas distributor in Ontario.

Retention of the gas system over many decades has proven a wise and popular decision spinning off in equitable rates, income for the municipality, and control of operating policies. The modern operations centre at 83 Elmsdale Drive and extensive distribution and service facilities comprise a considerable magnification of nineteenth-century origins.

The first "gas works" was started in 1883 as the Berlin Gas Company, a Breithaupt family firm producing manufactured gas from coal at its Gaukel Street plant. On June 1, 1903, the Berlin Light Commission bought the company, with 519 domestic, industrial, and street lighting clientele, for

$90,000. A decade later more than 2,000 gas customers were on file; by 1943 consumption topped 225 million cubic feet annually.

In the meantime the Kitchener P.U.C. re-affirmed a preference for the continuance of local ownership. "If our franchise is so valuable to an independent firm, why should we hand over such a large source of revenue to them and deprive the citizens of that money?" said Commissioner E. Saunder, quoted in the *Daily Record,* April 27, 1938.

In the early 1950s Alberta's abundant natural gas was clearly destined for Eastern Canada, and in 1957 the utility began supply negotiations. And again the local authorities opted to stay in business in the best interests of the community.

In May 1958 Kitchener began distributing natural gas to its customers; one month later the old manufactured gas plant was dismantled. With the introduction of regional government in 1973, gas distribution was no longer under a P.U.C., but became a division of the corporation of the City of Kitchener.

The dramatic growth of Kitchener Utilities in alliance with city government is further reflected by the consolidation of natural gas as a dependable, clean, and economic energy source. As the preferred choice for heating in 90 percent of new homes and for many industrial applications, gas is an accepted basic service in Kitchener as well as an element of merchandising potential. Virtually all of Kitchener Utilities vehicles operate on natural gas—700,000 vehicles worldwide and 20,000 in Canada—for reasons of improved air quality and cost savings. The utility has also met with success

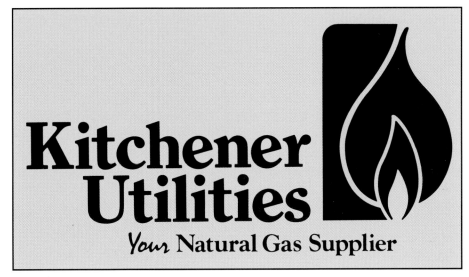

Kitchener Utilities

Your Natural Gas Supplier

in the rental of gas equipment and cultivated customer satisfaction with prompt, efficient service for all types of gas appliances.

In all of its endeavors, Kitchener Utilities exemplifies profitable independence consistent with the progressive spirit and community concern found in the city.

The water system in Kitchener also derived from private sources in the form of hand-dug wells that were prevalent in the 1870s, when Berlin's population was around the 3,000 mark. Water from Schneider's Creek was added for fire fighting until a municipal system was approved by referendum in 1887. Successful bidder Moffett, Hodgins & Clark of Syracuse, New York, built a pumping station at Shoemaker's Lake (now Greenbrook Park), constructed a 60,000-gallon standpipe on St. George Street (still the site of reservoir storage), and installed 6.5 miles of mains to supply 6,000 people. Later extended to Waterloo, the network served adequately for the 10-year term of the franchise.

In 1898 Kitchener purchased the system for $102,000, issuing 30-

year debentures at 3.75 percent. A board of commissioners was formed with J.C. Breithaupt as chairman, a post he held until 1948. Immediately the board encountered problems with contamination and frozen pipelines, but the board also installed eight wells and two miles of new mains in the first year to pump one million GPD to Berlin-Waterloo. Prophetically the annual report of 1899 declared,

Dependable potable water.

"It is not probable that the water supply of Berlin will ever be so abundant that reckless wastes can be permitted."

Initial major expansion in 1912 included the Duke Street standpipe, an MIG ground reservoir, and turbine pumps at Shoemaker. Then the Strange Street well field, reservoir, and pumping station were developed between 1920 and 1923, followed by wells in the Lancaster Street area in the late 1930s. Over the years the Grand River was considered as a source, even to the point of plans for a dam and filtration plant above Bridgeport in the mid-1940s, but it was not pursued at the time.

In 1949 four new wells were constructed in the Mannheim area, which with additional wells in Wilmot Township comprise a prime source of water for Kitchener. A reservoir constructed in 1957 receives the pumpage from the Mannheim well field and stores up to 11 MIG.

With the advent of regional government, the supply, storage, and trunk transmission of water was assigned to Waterloo Region with the cities responsible for local distribution. A regional priority on water supply has seen the implementation of induced infiltration wells from the Grand in 1979 and the current installation of the Mannheim Recharge system. Kitchener Utilities shares in the responsibility to promote wise use of water through conservation and demand management.

BREADNER TRAILER SALES INC.

A striking portrait of family corporate achievement identifies a fast-rising Kitchener enterprise with roots in the community that reach across the country.

Breadner Trailer Sales Inc. is scarcely a decade into well-calculated expansion, but it already claims leadership in the transportation industry as the largest independent trailer dealer in Canada. Its marketplace and service centres are strategically spaced from the Golden Horseshoe of Ontario to the capitals of western provinces.

Prior to growth in the 1980s, the company was a more localized operation centred at its current five-acre site at 10 Forwell Road. Founder Vernon Breadner of Kitch-

ener took the venture from a modest beginning in 1971 to a full-scale parts, service, and sales organization by the time of his death in 1981. At that juncture the business was recording $6 million in annual volume as control passed to sons Robert and Richard.

Second-generation management has produced spectacular results with the opening of a network of complete tractor/trailer depots at Calgary, Regina, and Winnipeg, as well as sales offices in Toronto and Edmonton. A leasing office and fleet of vehicles is also maintained at Breslau, Ontario.

The complement of highly trained personnel under the direction of president Robert Breadner has also widened to a total of 140 employees, including 35 at Kitchener headquarters and 28 to 35 people at each of the prairie locales. An increasingly important division of the firm is leasing, which accelerated after the 1988 acquisition of a major in the field, R&S Leasing of Kitchener.

Formation of a nationally positioned distribution company has seen Breadner Trailer Sales evolve into a well-recognized industry leader offering technical and finan-

With the opening of a network of complete tractor/trailer depots at Calgary, Regina, and Winnipeg as well as sales offices in Toronto and Edmonton, Breadner Trailer Sales has evolved into a well-recognized industry leader. Pictured here are (BELOW) an all-aluminum Wilson Livestock van and a Stoughton Dry Freight van (RIGHT).

cial assistance to its clients. In the view of the owners, the objectives in terms of response to transportation requirements are well advanced. Not only is their trailer line complete with an array of 360 vehicles in all van, flat deck, and livestock categories, but their leasing activity is meeting both short- and long-term needs.

Teamwork at Breadner Trailer Sales Inc. has also characterized the escalation to $40 million in sales annually. They are active in chamber of commerce and trucking associations, and Robert Breadner serves on the board of the Canadian Association of Family Enterprise.

ALLPRINT COMPANY LIMITED

Barely 15 years from inception, a progressive Kitchener printing house has more than fulfilled the founding aspirations of president Klaus Ertle in terms of expansion, modernization, and capability. Controlled growth has been accompanied by an uncompromising commitment to quality from the opening of Allprint Company Limited in a rented shop to the enviable environment and reputation enjoyed by 80 personnel in a 36,000-square-foot plant at 131 Shoemaker Street today. There, amid the hum of four-colour Heidelberg presses and the latest in typesetting, camera, and ancilliary equipment—some of it computer assisted—the graphic arts flourish.

Pacesetting always, Allprint is a striking example of the visual identity created so effectively for a widening roster of clients. When the firm occupied the present site in the fall of 1987, after an eight-year stand on Otonabee Drive, sole

Allprint's headquarters at 131 Shoemaker Street.

owner Ertle promoted the opening with a handsome binder illuminating not only the expertise of his enterprise but also the sometimes mysterious world of printing. Presently the company's creative leadership is adjusting to the complexities of innovative, electronic pre-press publishing systems.

Allprint's services transcend the spectrum of commercial printing in a market covering much of southern Ontario—and in the case of its label division, to customers in Vancouver and Montreal. Whether a major advertising agency in Toronto, a national distillery of long standing, or a fledgling small business, Allprint draws from resources anchored by a relentless attention to detail at every stage of production. Senior design and creative people work with all of the human and mechanical aids at their disposal and collaborate with the client to enhance the corporate image. The way in which the printed design is integrated to establish consumer confidence, suggest financial stability, and improve public

The Allprint management team: (from left) Warren Clarke, controller; Guenther Haas, vice president, operations; Bryan Lewcock, sales manager; and Klaus Ertle, president.

relations and marketing strength forms the benchmark of Allprint's success.

To further emboss an image, Allprint Company Limited offers extra dimensions of service, such as gold bronzing, promotion assembly, and coordination and distribution of materials. Die-cutting and bindery departments contribute to diverse configurations and finishes of printed product; superior sales support, service, and estimating allow for fast turn-around and quotations; the creative department brings an understanding of style, taste, typography, and layout to the design challenge.

On all counts—leadership in the printing sector, development of valued clientele, and an ideal workplace—the vision pursued by Klaus Ertle is continuing.

CONESTOGA COLD STORAGE LIMITED

The Kitchener facilities of Conestoga Cold Storage, a state-of-the-art food warehousing operation.

A state-of-the-art food warehousing facility opened in Kitchener just 15 years ago ranks today as one of the top three public cold storages in Ontario. Through several expansions of building and equipment, Conestoga Cold Storage Limited has established an enviable reputation for fast, efficient handling of a wide variety of perishable commodities. Its premises at 299 Trillium Drive now measure more than 3.7 million cubic feet, or seven times the original size. The model warehouse serves a large and diverse clientele that is predominantly in southern Ontario but also extends to the Pacific Rim.

A source of particular satisfaction to president Larry Laurin is the automated storage and retrieval system (AS/RS) functioning with computerized controls and some homemade technology within the plant to meet just-in-time delivery deadlines. Laurin and a compact management staff are comfortable with the computer-automated warehousing aspect of the operation.

Staged development of the company, which was founded in late 1974 on the present 19.3-acre site, was highlighted by erection of a $3.5-million, 80-foot-high refrigerated storage structure in 1979. This addition provided 1.5 million cubic feet, raising overall capacity to 2.3 million from an original 500,000 cubic feet. Complete with blast freezing unit, double-deep racking and stacker cranes, the towering edifice continues to handle a huge workload.

Innovation has also accompanied the development of Conestoga Cold Storage in the form of rack assemblies, conveyor refinements, and a re-piler, all designed by staff personnel. As a result the company maintains machine and maintenance shops to meet special requirements.

Laurin has also led the business into related fields in concert with the entry of new fresh or frozen meat and vegetables into the marketplace. The company specializes in clearances for imports and exports at its federally inspected premises. A companion company, Conestoga Franchise Services, supplies such well-known customers as the 75-outlet M&M Meats. Through the years Conestoga Cold Storage Limited has cultivated many long-term users of prominence, such as J.M. Schneider and National Grocers.

Laurin sees a bright future for his company as an economic route for food processors endeavoring to match its production with sales.

BECKERMANN EXQUISITE KITCHENS

Consummate craftsmanship and elegance in a functional format identify the distinctive kitchens created for a widening North American market by a flourishing Kitchener company. Beckermann Exquisite Kitchens blends European expertise with the ultimate in materials, equipment, and design to meet rising demand for its custom cabinetry and accessories. Five bright-green vans bearing the firm's logo move out in a continual procession from the Otanbee Drive plant with cargoes of contemporary and traditional kitchen assemblies destined for clients across Canada and in northern midwest and southeast U.S. regions.

President, founder, and sole owner Matthias Beckermann has watched his venture develop from a drawing-board concept in 1976 through several expansions to a

A stunning example of a custom-designed kitchen by Beckermann.

54,000-square-foot production facility, a second plant for warehousing and trimming at nearby Bleams Road, and several acres of land for future growth. Although well advanced with computer-assisted installations, Beckermann perpetuates standards of excellence inherited from a cabinet-making family and enhanced by a degree in wood and plastics engineering at the University of Rosenheim near Munich, Germany. His modular systems, whether upscale or old world, stunning or understated, are finished by the best European technology and personalized by a design team. A research and development unit responds to special situations, while hand tooling may be

One of the three Beckermann Kitchen Studios, large showrooms devoted exclusively to Beckermann kitchens.

applied prior to issuance of the customary lifetime warranty. As well, the firm offers more than 600 combinations of style, finish, and color, plus unlimited options in the areas of door handles and pulls, fume hoods, microwave shelves, and drawer arrangements.

As the leading business of its kind on the continent, Beckermann has also embarked on a successful associated enterprise, Beckermann Kitchen Studio, in partnership with the founder's brother-in-law, Pierre Bischoff. Since 1978 they have opened three large showrooms devoted exclusively to Beckermann kitchens. Recently the studios experienced patronage requiring six permanent sales people and an installation division to handle the increased volume. Apart from direct sales, a dealer network services the marketplace.

Presently Beckermann employs 70 highly qualified administrative and production workers to serve primarily a remodelling market valued at $1.7 billion annually in Canada alone. About 30 percent of output is exported to the United States which, added to increasing domestic sales, comprises an attractive future prospect for Beckermann Exquisite Kitchens custom-designed kitchens.

PATRONS

The following individuals, companies, and organizations have made a valuable commitment to the quality of this publication. Windsor Publications gratefully acknowledges their participation in *Kitchener: A Tradition of Excellence.*

Advance Metal Industries
   Limited*
Allprint Company Limited*
B&B Kieswetter Excavating Inc.*
Beckermann Exquisite Kitchens*
Bestpipe (A Division of Lake
   Ontario Cement Ltd.)
Breadner Trailer Sales Inc.*
Conestoga Cold Storage Limited*

Gateman-Milloy Inc.*
Hallman Group*
Kitchener Utilities*
Kuntz Electroplating Inc.*
Paragon Engineering Limited*
Proctor & Redfern Limited*
Rosen Industries Ltd.
Sowa Tool & Machine Co., Ltd.
Bonnie Stuart Shoes Limited*
The Walter Fedy Partnership*
Weston Bakeries*

*Participants in Part 2, "Kitchener's Enterprises." The stories of these companies and organizations appear in chapters 7 through 9, beginning on page 103.

Photo by Glen Jones

BIBLIOGRAPHY

NEWSPAPERS
Berlin News Record
Kitchener Daily Record
Kitchener Waterloo Record
Toronto Globe
Toronto Star

SOUVENIR PUBLICATIONS
Berlin: Celebration of Cityhood
   (1912)
Berlin Today (1906)
Busy Berlin (1890 and 1901)
Kitchener Centennial (1954)
Kitchener-Waterloo Profile (1987)
Kitchener-Waterloo Record,
   "Kitchener—125 Years" (1979)
Made in Berlin (1989)
Recollections of 125 Years (1979)

OTHER SOURCES
Bell, Nancy, et al. *Builders and*
   Boosters. Kitchener, 1986
Belobaba, Peter, et al. "Decision
   Making in the Urban Political
   System: The Kitchener Arts
   Centre Controversy." University
   of Waterloo paper, 1979.
Bunting, Trudi. "The Geography of
   Mainstreet." Department of
   Geography, University of
   Waterloo, 1984.
City of Kitchener. Business
   Development Department.
   "Kitchener: The Good Life."
English, John, and Kenneth
   McLaughlin. *Kitchener: An*
   Illustrated History. Waterloo,
   1983.
Hill, Nicholas. "King Street Facade
   Plan." June 1987.
Moyer, Bill. *Kitchener: Yesterday*
   Revisited. Burlington: Windsor
   Publications (Canada) Ltd.,
   1979.
————. *This Unique Heritage.*
   Kitchener, 1971.
Pasternak, Jack. *The Kitchener*
   Market Fight. Toronto, 1975.
Reive, T.G. "The Industrial
   Background of Waterloo County
   to 1914" B.A. Thesis, Waterloo

Lutheran University, 1970.
"A Special Report on the City of
   Kitchener." *Business and*
   Finance, February 1987.
Stanton, Raymond. *A Legacy of*
   Quality: J.M. Schneider Inc., A
   Centennial Celebration.
   Kitchener, 1989.
Steiner, Samuel J. *Vicarious*
   Pioneer: The Life of Jacob Y.
   Shantz. Winnipeg, 1988.
Stroh, Jacob. "Reminiscences of
   Berlin." *Waterloo Historical*
   Society 66 (1978).
Uttley, W.V. *A History of Kitchener,*
   Ontario. Waterloo, 1937.
Walker, David F. *Manufacturing in*
   Kitchener-Waterloo: A Long
   Term Perspective. Waterloo,
   1987.

DIRECTORY OF CORPORATE SPONSORS

Advance Metal Industries Limited,
114-115
133 Dundas Street
Post Office Box 245
Kitchener, Ontario N2G 3X9
519/742-0211
Barry Gilders

Allprint Company Limited, 127
131 Shoemaker Street
Kitchener, Ontario N2E 3B5
519/748-5120
Klaus Ertle

B&B Kieswetter Excavating Inc.,
111
1801 Bleams Road
Kitchener, Ontario N2G 3W5
519/578-0070
Bob Kieswetter

Beckermann Exquisite Kitchens,
129
44 Otonabee Drive
Kitchener, Ontario N2C 1L6
519/893-6280
Matthias Beckermann

Breadner Trailer Sales Inc., 126
10 Forwell Road
Kitchener, Ontario N2B 3E7
519/576-9290
Robert Breadner

Conestoga Cold Storage Limited, 128
299 Trillium Drive
Kitchener, Ontario N2E 1W9
519/748-5415
Larry Laurin

Gateman-Milloy Inc., 106-107
270 Shoemaker Street
Kitchener, Ontario N2E 3E1
519/748-6500
Mike Milloy

Hallman Group, 109
230 Gage Avenue
Kitchener, Ontario N2M 2C8
519/742-5841
Lyle S. Hallman

Kitchener Utilities, 124-125
83 Elmsdale Drive
Post Office Box 1118
Kitchener, Ontario N2G 4G7
519/741-2530
E.S. Kovacs

Kuntz Electroplating Inc., 116-117
851 Wilson Avenue
Kitchener, Ontario N2C 1J1
519/893-7680
Robert Germann

Paragon Engineering Limited, 108
871 Victoria Street North, Suite 300
Kitchener, Ontario N2B 3S4
519/579-4410
Ray Alarie

Proctor & Redfern Limited, 110
41 George Street South
Brampton, Ontario L6Y 2E1
416/450-0900
Grant Lee

Bonnie Stuart Shoes Limited, 120
141 Whitney Place
Kitchener, Ontario N2G 3Y9
519/578-8880
Cameron Stuart

The Walter Fedy Partnership, 104-
105
546 Belmont Avenue West
Post Office Box 368
Kitchener, Ontario N2G 3Y9
519/576-5499
Roger Farwell

Weston Bakeries, 118-119
560 Victoria Street North
Kitchener, Ontario N2H 5H2
519/742-4491
John King

INDEX

Italicized numbers indicate illustrations